Brislington
Ghosts
and
Mysteries

Brislington Ghosts and Mysteries

KEN TAYLOR

redcliffe

Dedication

This book is dedicated to the people of Brislington past, present and future and, especially, to Jonathan Rowe whose devotion to the heritage of the parish has preserved so much of value, and in memory of his father Norman Rowe who passed away as the final touches were being made to the manuscript: his strength of purpose benefited a great many lives, reminding us that whether or not our spirit survives – our influence certainly does.

First published in 2005 by Redcliffe Press Ltd.,
81g Pembroke Road, Bristol BS8 3EA

ISBN 1 904537 38 3

British Library Cataloguing-in-Publication Data
A catalogue record for this book is available from the British Library

Design and typesetting by Stephen Morris Communications, smc@freeuk.com
Printed and bound by MPG Books Ltd., Bodmin, Cornwall

The following photographs are reproduced with kind permission from:
Dee Roberts: Lilian, page 29
Joules Taylor: St Anne's Well, page 51
Memories: Langton Court Hotel, page 22 and detail of ghost, page 23 (digital enhancement and tracing by Joules Taylor)
Vicki Trotman: New Year's celebration, page 14, detail of orb page 16, and Highworth Road orb, page 16 (digital enhancements of orbs by Ken Taylor)
All other photographs and drawings are by Ken Taylor.

Contents

Acknowledgements

I would like to thank everyone who has contributed to this project and, in particular, the following:
Adrian Good, Alan Woodward, Ann Bird, Bruce Boorer, Christine Bowles, Darren Mann, Denis Plunkett, Dorothy Brewer, Edward Sutor, Eunice Rowe, Gary Milward, Helen Monteiro De Lima, Jonathan Rowe, Joules Taylor, Julie Fernandez, June Travanti, Kai Taylor, Karen Kane, Kerrie Travanti, Lesley Owens, Louise Noon, Mary Mitchell, Mel Twogood, Paul Munden, Phi Tran, Phil Quinn, Richard Coupe, Richard Heaton, Rosemary Gough, Sharon Barr, Simon Williams, Stu Neville, Terry O'Sullivan, Teresa Boorer, Trevor Kane, Vera Payne, Veronica Pollard, and Vicki Trotman.

Disclaimer

These stories are offered in good faith as true: the author has researched them as rigorously as practical, and to the best of his knowledge they are true in the sense that each witness has described an actual experience. However, the very nature of the paranormal makes it impossible to claim that these stories are 'true' in the conventional sense of established fact (the English legal system, for example, is rigorous in its official disbelief in ghosts). Therefore the interpretation of the experiences is open to question, and no warranty can be given regarding the empirical existence of ghosts, UFOs, or other paranormal phenomena.

If you think you may have a problem, seek suitably qualified help. But remember, supernatural events of whatever sort are rare – very rare – so don't have nightmares.

Foreword

TRYSTAN SWALE

RESEARCHER: SEVERNSIDE CENTRE FOR FORTEAN RESEARCH

Like many dedicated investigators of paranormal phenomena, I have a strong interest in the work of Charles Fort (1874–1932). This New York-based author dedicated much of his life to chronicling reports of anomalous and bizarre events.

His most famous legacy is a single quote, which seems as apt today as it was at the time it was written: 'one measures a circle, beginning anywhere'. This statement came in the context that it is impossible to make general conclusions as to the cause of ghosts, monsters and other fantastic creatures. Quite simply, Fort discovered that the study of those mysterious visitors he termed 'the damned' produced far more questions than answers.

The most obvious question of all is 'what are these things?' – a query which has seen authors such as Colin Wilson and T C Lethbridge churn out reams of content in search of an explanation without pinning down the truth. Parapsychologists continue to be surprised by their experiments, even when they feel they are close to proving that the human mind holds the answer. Finally, there are investigators such as myself and my SCFR colleagues who may be able to reassure witnesses of their sanity, yet acknowledge that sometimes we do not possess all the answers. At present that circle remains too large to handle, and anyone who claims he has found its beginning and end may need to reassess his beliefs.

Fort himself was not interested in producing any theories of his own, and I would certainly argue that this has helped secure his legacy through the decades. Yet many of his critics rightly conclude that Fort's most basic error was a failure to acknowledge that witness testimony can be flawed or even hoaxed. Within the pages of this book, Fort's greatest weakness is Ken Taylor's major strength: evidence is analysed with an unbiased mind. You, the reader, have the chance to draw your own conclusions as to reality and myth.

Choose carefully and this book may guide you on a curved route towards both beginning and end.

Introduction

Ghosts, like teenagers, tend to provoke strong reactions in all but the most tolerant souls. During the ten years I have been researching this book I've met people who insist ghosts should be neither seen nor heard, while others instinctively reach out in friendship to their otherworldly neighbours.

Surveys suggest half the British population believes in psychic phenomena, but English law neither recognises the existence of ghosts, nor affords them any legal rights whatsoever, and the Church traditionally regards them as unhealthy, even diabolical. Yet the stories I have collected reflect real experiences honestly told, and clearly reveal that ghosts seem to display distinctly human characteristics. Imagine you became a ghost one day – how would you like to be treated?

So, can anyone see ghosts, or is there a sort of 'psychic gene' only certain people have? Well, the same could be asked about people who watch football or gardening programmes. Although few of us could become professional footballers, landscape designers, or psychics, we can all play ball, arrange a better bit of greenery, or see something anomalous from time to time.

With so many publications devoted to local history and our natural history, I thought it was high time there should be a book on Brislington's supernatural history. With a topic this broad, ranging from ghosts to UFOs, and from superstition to religion, this neighbourhood offers enough material to fill many volumes, but I trust this one will help restore the balance.

Perhaps this offering will encourage more people to share their experiences with each other, so that the strangeness of these incidents will be eroded, and the similarities between them become increasingly apparent. Once we learn to recognise the connections we may be closer to finding the origin/s of these enduring mysteries.

At the very least this anthology of new and traditional tales offers an insight into a side of Brislington normally overlooked, and perhaps opens a window onto a dimension usually hidden from view. I am content to have recorded the evidence, and am grateful to John Sansom of Redcliffe Press for publishing it; all that is left is for you to enjoy making up your mind as to what it all means.

Ghosts

Hicks Gate House
Hicks Gate

Royalist soldiers may have been harboured here in the Civil War, and the infamous Judge Jeffries is also rumoured to have stayed here in 1685, year of the Bloody Assizes, but these tales may merely be romantic legends, as in the seventeenth century the building was fairly humble and scarcely fit for distinguished guests.

Another story says the house, which is on the Bristol to London road, once served as a coaching inn and that somebody was murdered in one of the upstairs guest bedrooms. This room was to feature in a haunting that occurred in the early 1920s when the Gough family lived at the house. I am very grateful to Rosemary Gough, granddaughter of householders Harold and Edith Gough for sharing her lucid memories of the story as it was handed down to her about sixty years ago.

The Gough family had lived there since 1914; Harold was the first headmaster of the Lower School at Bristol Grammar School, while his wife Edith ran their home and bred wire-haired fox terriers. The house comprised two storeys and an attic which was used mainly for storage but also gave access to a little room beside the road, believed to have been occupied by a servant. A small, rather dark staircase connected the first floor and attic, which were to be the focus of the haunting. The house had neither electricity nor gas, so candles and small oil-lamps were the only lighting available.

'One day', Rosemary wrote to me, 'some of the dogs were digging in the garden, as was their wont, when one of them turned up a human skull. I don't know what the reaction of the family was, but I was told that it was put into the apple room. There was a door at the back of the house facing the garden, which opened into a small room, with no window or door into the rest of the house. There were slatted shelves on three sides and these were used for storing apples through the winter. It was on these shelves that the skull was placed, and the door was shut. The following day, someone would walk into Keynsham to seek the advice of the vicar for its burial.

'That night the family went to bed as usual and all were asleep. In the early hours of the morning they were woken by footsteps coming down the stairs from the attic and walking to the end of a long passage, past a small bedroom[1] and on to the two large bedrooms at the end [these included the bedroom in which the story had said that someone had been murdered]. It was heard to

---

1. Occupied by their daughter Marjorie, a young woman at the time, who ran a small school at the house.

Tombstone in St Luke's churchyard

turn one of the handles of the doors before returning along the passage and up the stairs to the attic.

'Next morning it transpired that they had all heard this in the night, but had thought that it was another member of the household moving around and had turned over and gone back to sleep. No one, however, had been out of their room that night! That morning the skull was placed in the hands of the vicar who, I believe, gave it a Christian burial in consecrated ground.'

All was then quiet once more at Hicks Gate House.

In 2005 I contacted the current owners, John and Bridget Pursey. They had moved into the house in 1977 and shortly afterwards, during renovations, 'John felt someone was looking over his shoulder, someone who had lived in the house and loved the house, making sure he [John] was doing what he should be doing.' Bridget emphasised that it 'was not a bad feeling.'

She also mentioned John had felt there were 'people walking along corridors', and noticed there were 'doors opening and shutting' without explanation. Perhaps most tellingly of all, their black Irish Wolfhound-cross would happily walk upstairs to the first-floor landing, but would refuse to go along the passageway there.

They have become so accustomed to incidents in the house, that whenever anything untoward happens, they refer to it lightheartedly as 'Charlie' doing it. An outstanding example of live-and-let-live.

Keepers Cottage
Brislington Hill

Keepers Cottage is a charming seventeenth-century building largely shielded from the busy A4 Bath Road by a mature copper beech tree planted in the neighbouring property around 1899 by Mrs Sherwell to commemorate the birth of their eldest son. It has been occupied by members of the Mitchell family since 1954 and I am grateful to Mary, the present owner, for sharing information with me.

Brislington suffered many air raids during the Second World War, and

Keepers Cottage was damaged, with the roof tiles being 'shuffled up like a pack of cards' by blast from a bomb that fell on nearby Brislington Hill House. It has been suggested that this structural disturbance may have somehow triggered the first known apparitions.

Mary only learned of this during a visit from Ann Dalby whose family were living at the cottage at the time, when she said 'Did you know you had a ghost? It was seen by my mother and my aunt several times on the upstairs landing.'

That same afternoon Mary's younger son Gerry called in and she told him what Ann had said. To her great surprise Gerry said that years before when he was aged about seven, he had been sitting at the dining room table doing his homework when 'a person in light' came in through the door.

'A person in light' was Gerry's own description, and she was reluctant to press him for more details because she did not want to influence what she would be told. This is a particularly sensitive observation that many would-be researchers would do well to respect.

The doorway through which the figure emerged connects the living room with the kitchen, which is located at the rear of the house on a slightly lower level. However, the door would originally have been an external entrance as the kitchen was possibly a mid-nineteenth century addition. There was no natural source for any such light to appear.

This event also may be connected with an upheaval in the fabric of the building – renovation work had been carried out to strengthen the ceiling beam in the living room itself.

Mary herself was fortunate enough to have an encounter of a particularly homely and comforting type. It was summer in the early 1990s, and she was working in the garden when she had a strong feeling that she was not alone. 'Just for an instant there was a figure standing in the flower border!'

Although some people might scoff at this sort of incident, considering it to be rather vague and insubstantial, a 'presence' can be perceived as being just as real as a flesh and blood person right beside you. And, yet again, something had been done to the house – major roof repairs after gales that year.

This unusual, yet benign, sequence of manifestations seems to demonstrate a concern for the well-being of the cottage, only appearing during times of structural crisis when things are disturbed, particularly the roof area. However, despite its proximity to the busy modern road, this house is characterised by a spirit of enduring tranquillity.

Hardwick Close

Before the houses of Hardwick Close were built, the land was an orchard which, according to local legend, had formerly belonged to Newycke (later Wick House) and therefore was part of the large medieval holdings run by the Chapel of St Anne in the Woods.

The story goes that a monk committed suicide in the immediate vicinity and, as suicide is a sin in the eyes of the Church, his soul was denied the heavenly peace his vocation had promised him. His unquiet spirit is said to still haunt the area, although he seems to have calmed down a lot since the troubles that made news in the early 1960s.

In 2005 I spoke with Irene Ranahan who has lived in Hardwick Close for 43 years. She told me that between 1962 and 1963 a poltergeist caused disturbances at a house near School Road where a middle-aged couple lived. The woman particularly loved knitting.

'One morning she came downstairs to find her work all unravelled and wound back up into a ball with the needles stuck into it. She assumed it was a prank of some sort, and didn't take much notice, but a couple of days later she came downstairs in the morning and all the pictures from her hall and lounge were propped up in the hall.'

None of the pictures had been damaged in the slightest, but of course her knitting was utterly destroyed. These two inexplicable events recurred several times during the next few weeks, and the deepening sense of unease and mystery badly affected her nerves.

The Reverend Osmund Moss (vicar of St Luke's Church from 1955 to 1966) was called in to free the household from its distressing and unnatural ordeal. His activities were successful in exorcising the ghost from the house but it seems the monk didn't exchange the earthly realm for any celestial abode and merely moved into another home further along the Close.

Irene calls him her 'happy ghost', adding 'every night he walks across our ceiling of the lounge, in our front bedroom, running almost: creak, creak, creak.' This is usually between 7.30pm and 8pm, and he often returns five minutes later; sometimes this to-ing and fro-ing occurs several times, when she says he is 'out to play'.

Anyone sceptical may find it easy to dismiss the creaking as the result of thermal contraction as the exterior of the house cools in the evening, combined perhaps with some expansion of the interior as heating comes on. However, I found Irene to have a wealth of common sense, many friends, and she plays an active role in the community: all in all an unlikely candidate for such a simple self-deception.

There was also a much more remarkable event when both she and her husband saw something that is still imprinted vividly on their memories, despite it taking mere seconds and happening 25 years ago. It was shortly after 12.30 at night, and they were settling down to bed. Roger noticed it first – a presence by Irene's side of the bed. It moved around the foot of the bed and out of the open door. Then they both saw 'a quick flash of white light' rapidly descend the stairs. They looked at each other in amazement as if to say 'Did you see that?'. It had no distinct shape – Roger simply described it as a blob, but Irene thought its lower half was bulbous and tapering towards the top, somewhat like a candle flame.

Roger said everything in the room went cold afterwards, adding 'no way I was going to get out of bed and follow it!' Irene however, felt the atmosphere in the room was unusually warm after the visitation.

There has never been even a hint of poltergeist activity in the house, and the spirit seems to live there contentedly – a welcome if rarely glimpsed long-term guest.

Highworth Road
St Anne's

In January 2005 a young woman who wishes to be anonymous – we shall call her Nicola – found my website more than usually interesting, and contacted me. She had been experiencing some weird phenomena at her home in Highworth Road and was looking for an explanation.

She had lived in the house for well over a year with her partner and young child, and had become increasingly concerned about unsettling events, but when she saw some photographs of herself taken during the yuletide festivities she promptly decided to investigate matters.

She told me: 'There have been times when I have gone to bed and heard unexplained bangs and knocking noises. I have gone to find out where these noises are coming from and found that everyone in my house was sound asleep. There have been other times when we have woken up in the morning to find all the wardrobe doors wide open, knowing they were all closed when we have gone to bed. Other times lights have gone on and off on their own...'

Apart from this mild poltergeist activity, she was also often troubled by the uneasy feeling that someone – or something – was watching her, particularly on the stairway and in the lower hall. Nicola's partner, who was sceptical about ghosts and the like, had also experienced similar sensations.

A photograph taken on the evening of December 29th in the lower hallway of her home showed some abnormalities that seemed to tie-in with those uncanny feelings: above her, and to her left and right were small circles of light – and a fourth was right in front of her, clearly visible against black clothes.

Another, taken a few days later at Westbury-on-Trym, minutes into the New Year, revealed no fewer than six of these mysterious circles. She sent them to me asking for my opinion, seeking 'a simple explanation for these strange little lights'.

Most of the orbs were so faint that I only found them using one of the specialist software packages used to create digital art, but two were reasonably easy to find in the photograph. There is a large one at the top right hand corner, and there is one directly in front of Nicola who is in the centre wearing a black top.

These lights are much discussed by parapsychologists, who call them 'orbs', a term coined by Dr Dave Oester in 1994 to describe the shape of the photographic anomaly. I decided to seek an expert opinion and contacted Adrian Good, whose wide experience and skill in the photographic arts (both film and digital) qualified him to consider factors that are a quantum leap beyond the scope of the layman such as myself.

Orbs of light

After discounting a permanent flaw with the lens (the orbs do not appear in the same positions), Adrian examined the photograph, and reported that 'Apart from the obvious 'red-eye' effect in all of the subjects in the picture caused by the integral flash being set close to the lens axis, the camera has recorded a faithful image'.

He went on to say: 'Highlights or 'hot-spots' are evident in the glass framed picture behind the group as a result of flash bouncing off the glass. I do not see that this could generate an effect of the mysterious spheres.'

He also explained that even if the camera lens is a 35mm wide-angle and of fixed aperture (causing exaggerated perspectives) 'it still doesn't explain the disparate sizes of the "orbs".'

However, he did not categorically discount the possibility that dust floating in the air near the camera could produce an out-of-focus blob when illuminated by the brilliance of the flash. Such dust may come from a wide range of everyday sources including clothing or the party poppers used in Nicola's New Year's Eve celebrations – the smoke particles would be too fine to produce any discrete images, but fragments of paper dust etc could linger in the air and reflect specks of light.

Orbs are controversial: people who believe in ghosts interpret them as ghosts; people who have faith in angels believe orbs are angelic; people who think occultism is evil regard them as demonic; people interested in psychokinesis think they're emanations of our own mental energy; and people who do not believe in the supernatural simply call them dust.

Given this range of interpretations, I have a good deal of sympathy for the notion that spiritual truth may be impossible for any mind of flesh and blood to comprehend, ever, but that shouldn't stop us trying. In fact, if you believe in spirituality at all, you have to accept the possibility that signs could be tailored to the level of understanding of the person they are intended to enlighten: perhaps, somehow, one person's mote of dust could be another person's spirit guide. After all, light itself is simultaneously particle and wave – in clear defiance of common sense – so why shouldn't enlightenment also manifest in paradox?

Each photograph shows an orb directly in front of Nicola (these are the ones illustrated; note that contrast and brightness have been optimised to show the orbs' internal features). That is a striking coincidence, tempting us to think the orbs have a message meant for her personally. Was it merely coincidence the lovely arc of orbs in the pub was suggestive of an angel's protective wing? It must be said that such speculations are in the same tradition of symbolism as

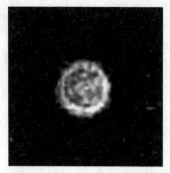

Enlargements of the hallway orb (*left*) and the public house orb (*right*)

the fortune-teller's art of tea leaf reading. However, an incident soon afterwards gave Nicola pause for thought.

On the morning of January 4th she was driving on the M5 when 'all of a sudden a massive black metal box came flying from the car in front, and hit our car'. She was shocked and very scared, but it wasn't until she saw the damage done to her car bonnet that she realised 'had we have been going a little faster and a bit closer to the car in front, the box would have come straight through the windscreen and cut us all to pieces. This may sound silly, but it makes me wonder, were those orbs around us, protecting us in some way?'

The human mind instinctively tries to make connections between events and ideas – that's how we all start to learn – so it's perfectly natural to wonder whether there is a link between the accident and the orbs. Indeed, this mental ability is very powerful and makes it almost inevitable that anyone bereaved and grief-stricken would assume a timely orb was a manifestation of the spirit of their dear departed. Likewise, many people in times of crisis become convinced that orbs are angelic beings that protect, nurture and comfort them.

Some researchers would wholeheartedly support the idea that the orbs clustering around Nicola demonstrate the presence of her personal guardian angel, shielding her from the worst-case scenario of the road traffic accident. Such interpretations appeal to many people who choose to believe them as a matter of faith, even if it does require some pretty big assumptions about the nature of the spirit world.

Within a week of Nicola's first contacting me, paranormal activity slowed to a level that was tolerable. This is not unusual – it's as if the troubles arise from the spirit resenting being ignored and, once its presence is recognised, a kind of truce ensues.

In April Nicola wrote to me saying: 'Everything seemed to go very quiet and all was absolutely fine in the house, there were no lights switching on and off, no strange noises, no unwanted feelings etc, however everything has changed in the last couple of days...'

On April 17th, about 8pm she had gone upstairs to the bathroom, and 'as I was reaching the top of the stairs there was a really really icy cold spot (bearing in mind we had the heating on full blast since around 4pm), I carried on up and as I reached the top and was on the landing, the coldness had gone.'

Although the cold spot was still there when she returned downstairs, she didn't mention it to her partner but... 'A while later my partner went up, and came shooting down the stairs all flustered and upset, when I asked her what was wrong she said "there is a really cold spot on the stairs, did you feel it?" I told her I had felt it too.'

'As the night went on the coldness was still there but it seemed to be moving up and down the stairs, one minute it would be right at the top and when you passed it a minute later it had moved down a little. What baffled me was the fact that it was the only place in the house that felt icy (our house is always like a sauna).'

Worse was to come. Late that same evening, after just a couple of hours sleep, Nicola awoke to her partner's caress: 'I was stirred by my partner wrapping herself around me to cuddle me in, and all of a sudden my head started pounding and fuzzing like a migraine, I must have woken up and as I sat up in tears from the pain I realised that my partner was fast asleep and had her back to me.'

In fact that's only half the story, as this nightmare encounter had culminated in an incident that would not be out of place in a tale of incubus assault. Monday was blighted by feelings of upset, tiredness and depression. And on Tuesday the cold spot on the stairs returned.

But although she was suffering increasing persecution with courage and determination, events were moving around her, events that would offer her a remarkable hope of support and relief. On that same Tuesday I was contacted by the BBC. They wanted to film a medium at work, someone who specialised in helping earthbound spirits move onto a more purely spiritual existence – did I know of anyone with a troublesome ghost they'd prefer to live without?

Most of the people I knew who had active hauntings actually wanted to keep their ghosts, but I drew up a shortlist and ranked them in order of priority. One case stood head and shoulders above the others because the household included an infant daughter.

About two years ago (when the haunting began) Nicola's daughter had inexplicably become distressingly fearful of sleeping – for fully three months she cried herself to sleep – and at that time she had also sat in her bedroom speaking to a man no one else could see. Just an imaginary friend perhaps, but with all the recent goings-on, Nicola began to doubt the explanation was that simple or benign.

Although she would have preferred a scientific investigation by experienced researchers into the paranormal, rather than a cleansing by a medium, in the wake of her terrifying nocturnal ordeal, Nicola accepted the offer. So, on the evening of April 28th the crew from the long-running Sunday morning BBC1 show *Heaven and Earth* arrived in Highworth Road.[1]

Presenters Matt Allwright and Julie Fernandez (on the right of the photograph, with Matt beside her) interviewed Nicola and her partner and discussed the supernatural events that had been causing the problems. Then self-styled 'soul rescuer' Terry O'Sullivan arrived. He explained that he would normally start at the cellar and work his way up through the house, but in this instance he already knew where the psychic hotspot was: he started work on the stairs where the cold spot had been encountered so many times.

Halfway up he called out to the spirit and noted an echo that he said the ghost had been using as an energy source to turn back against the family. He took this discovery in his stride and continued up to the landing. Closing in on the spirit, Terry revealed that the ghost was that of a man who had once lived in the house, and was harassing the family to get them to move out.

On the first floor, Julie started questioning the medium about the reasons for the haunting. The ghost began speaking through Terry and in a high, almost cracking voice, and in staccato sentences blurted out that he hated living with the women (Nicola, her daughter, and partner). Julie repeatedly but benevolently pressed him for a reason why. He hated all women. Why? Because his mother had beaten him.

Terry tried to convince the man, who appeared to be an elderly man wearing 1950s-60s clothes and felt he still owned the house, that he should leave. Then Terry conjured the 'paradise path' a psychic link to heaven that could enable the man's predecessors to greet him, and he was guided into the light.

Julie and the team returned to Highworth Road the following week to conclude the segment with an update. Nicola confirmed that all phenomena had ceased but she still felt there was a presence in the house. Julie mentioned to me that those impressions were probably a sort of psychic residue that would dis-

---

1. Broadcast on BBC1 May 29th, 2005.

The BBC *Heaven and Earth* presenters with the family at Highworth Road

sipate soon, and Terry later confirmed that the original filming had run so late he didn't have time to re-energise the house, so the fading echoes of the earthbound spirit were still being felt instead of being cleansed outright.

Nicola's partner, who had always been sceptical, confessed that the exorcism had opened her eyes about ghosts. Shortly after Terry had reached the top of the stairs and was confronting the spirit, she had felt a physical sensation as if she had been poked in the stomach (Matt considered this a perfectly natural reaction to the tension Terry had built up during his dramatic ritual).

Fortunately, fully six weeks later when this manuscript was being completed ready for publication, Nicola assured me the household had remained untroubled by further disturbance.

Incidentally, Nicola's anxiety had been heightened early on in the sequence of the above events when, searching the internet for an insight into the history of her home, she found a reference to an exorcism in Highworth Road[1]. I duly contacted the website owner and Darren Mann kindly gave me the source of the story. The published information was meagre, though: the Reverend FJW Maddock, who was vicar of St Anne's church from 1949 to 1956, conducted an exorcism at one of houses to free it from the unwelcome attentions of the ghost of an old lady.[2]

Wick Road

To protect the privacy of its present occupiers, I have preserved the anonymity of this troubled house, within whose walls an earthbound spirit put a young family through a terrifying ordeal.

1. Darren Mann 2005, www.paranormaldatabase.com/somerset/somedata.php?pageNum _paradata=1 [accessed 17.06.05].

2. Dennis Barden 1965, *Ghosts & Hauntings*, London, Zeus Press.

To look at, it seems to be a perfectly ordinary late Victorian / early Edwardian mid-terrace property, typical of the many buildings erected when Bristol's land-hungry borders encroached into the fields that once surrounded the village of Brislington. But it seems that maybe something in its history left an alarming legacy that lingered somehow, unseen and unsuspected through the years.

In the weeks before Christmas 1995, a spate of uncanny incidents culminated in a horrifying ordeal for an 11-year-old girl – Kerrie Travanti.

Typical poltergeist phenomena included:

- A light suspended from the ceiling at the bottom of the stairs moved up and down (not side to side) on its flex.
- A bathroom hot tap repeatedly turned on by itself.
- A baby monitor intercom that had been left securely plugged into its socket was found lying in the middle of the nursery.
- A sturdy Father Christmas decoration unfastened itself from a door, and floated across the room 'like it was made of tissue paper'.
- Christmas cards set in a stand were found one morning to have been bent down...

    ...all except one. The only card left undamaged was from Kerrie to her sister Michelle who was renting the house.

On the night of December 11th, Kerrie was staying with her sister and by about 11.30pm was in bed in an upstairs bedroom at the back of the house. That's when she saw a figure appear in a corner of the room.

She described it to me as 'a man with long black hair down his back, short on the top and spiky.' She could see the top part of his torso but 'no arms and no legs'. The figure seemed to be 'fading in and out' and looming towards her and then receding.

Kerrie panicked: she tried to scream but couldn't make a sound. It was as if she were frozen. The room was small, with the bed occupying most of the space, so the only way to get to the door was to actually head towards the ghost. Kerrie plucked up courage and 'got up and went through him, and ran downstairs.'

Michelle's boyfriend David was in the kitchen at the time, and reported a sensation of cold that seemed to emanate from above his head – the kitchen is immediately below the bedroom where Kerrie had her petrifying encounter.

Kerrie left the house that night.

Anyone familiar with ghost lore will have nodded knowingly at the list of physical disturbances: those sorts of paranormal activity are often reported in haunted households where there is a girl of approximately Kerrie's age. The standard theory about poltergeists suggests that the emotional turmoil of adolescence can produce enough psychic energy to either trigger phenomena latent in the building, or even to create a brand new disturbance.

In the latter case the paranormal events are reckoned to be the manifestation of the girl's own spontaneous telekinesis, and are not indicative of a conventional ghost. Of course, in those very rare cases where the living and the dead start feeding off each other's energy, the situation is explosive, sparking the most extreme and dangerous forms of poltergeist activity. Here, though, the evidence from later witnesses argues against Kerrie being unwittingly responsible.

The following evening, at around 5.30 pm (it was already dark), their mother June went to the house. She hadn't heard the details of the events but when she entered the bedroom and looked into the corner where Kerrie had seen the ghost, she 'visualised... a man's head with a white shroud on it.'

June told Kerrie about her vision, at which the girl became distraught, crying 'Don't say that!' The confirmation of her own experience proved almost too much to bear.

The family felt out of their depth, and looked for help. They contacted the vicar of St Anne's Church, and he duly visited the house to bless it, paying particular attention to the bathroom and the bedroom. When it was finished he told June that during the blessing he saw the spirit of the man.

A week later he returned and performed the ceremony again. June recalls 'He said he could feel the spirit around him... He couldn't remove it.'

It seems he was right, because after Michelle vacated the premises, a girlfriend of Kerrie's moved in with another female friend and later said they too had experienced similar disturbances.

About the ghost himself, June clearly remembers the vicar saying 'He just needed help ... He was stuck and wanted Kerrie to talk to him.' Hopefully by now this tardy tenant has learned to communicate without scaring people half out of their wits, and has moved from these premises to somewhere more suitable.

Langton Court Hotel
Langton Court Road

Built on the site of the demolished Tudor mansion Langton Court, the Langton Court Hotel opened for business in 1902, and is now run as a public house – its cellars being a survival from the earlier building.

Several early photographs survive of this building with its ornate and attractive facade. One is displayed in the bar and was shown to me by landlady

Lesley Owens – it clearly shows a ghostly figure inside the left hand doorway under the columns, she is seen in profile facing to the right[1]. She stands in shadow, ignored by everyone else in the photograph, yet is quite clearly defined with long fair hair gathered behind her neck, and a long white dress, perhaps leaning on a parasol as the tracing indicates.

There is something about the figure that immediately distances it from the robust postures of the men, and it seemed to me that she was more likely to be an optical illusion than a woman physically present at the time of the photograph. But then, just because photographs of ghosts are notoriously unreliable, that doesn't automatically mean they are all illusions. Certainly there are people happy to believe she is indeed a spirit.

Three other ghosts have been reported at the hotel in recent years. In autumn 2003 a visiting psychic from Swindon entered the extension (to the right of the main bar) and he felt the presence of a Victorian man who 'overdosed on opium'.

Lesley told me, 'he said the guy had not passed over and was scared.' Embarking on an impromptu mid-day exorcism, the medium sat on the floor at

The Langton Court Hotel

22   1. Photograph reproduced with kind permission of Memories, St Nicholas Market, Corn Street, Bristol.

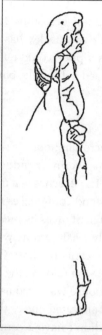

The Langton Court Hotel ghost appears in this photograph that hangs in the bar. On the right, the traced shape of the apparition

the bottom of the steps, placed his hands palm up on his knees, and explained to the spirit how 'there would be other people waiting for him'.

With this encouragement the ghost promptly left the earthly plane. Lesley vividly recalls how, despite the medium's hands remaining open on his knees, 'the veins popped on his arms'. She later checked the history of the spot and found that until the extension was built in 1981 it had been a courtyard. However, she recalled the medium suggesting that it could be the site – not the building – that was haunted.

Another ghost seems to belong to a different class of haunting: instead of being a living spirit trapped on earth, it seems to be a mere reflection or shadow cast through time. An image of something no longer there. At the opposite end of the main bar from the extension is a gents' lavatory and here 'a little boy' in a 'cap, peaked like a schoolboy's' has been seen a couple of times by one of the cleaners but always only as 'a quick glance out of the corner of her eye'. There was never any uncomfortable feeling at these occasions, and no sense of presence whatsoever.

In the last couple of years an upstairs room has been rented to a judo club, and one of the members told Lesley about an old man with grey hair he had seen in the doorway behind the bar. He was wearing modern clothes. The witness has seen the figure on a few occasions, from a seat along the outside wall directly in front of that doorway. Lesley has checked, and there is no single historical person that this description could refer to, but it certainly does not relate to any person then employed behind the bar.

The Beeches
Broomhill Road

This large, early-Victorian house is set in 22 acres of grounds and has an air of elegance as well as a warm, friendly atmosphere. With many original features carefully retained, The Beeches is a unique and popular venue for events ranging from weddings and conferences to murder mystery weekends.

Apparently, though, it owes its present tranquillity to an exorcism carried out in the 1980s or early 1990s, a time when the South West Gas Board owned the building. In 2004 I met Sharon Barr, General Manager of The Beeches Hotel and Conference Centre, who told me the story as it had been handed down to her.

At the time, the house was used as a Training Centre, and an executive from the Gas Board was allocated one of the upstairs bedrooms to stay in overnight. Unfortunately, he didn't have a comfortable night. In fact he practically 'Had the life frightened out of him'.

He was visited by the ghost of 'Jake', a young man who had worked at the house when it was the home of Dr Charles Henry Fox (son of Dr Francis Fox, q.v.), a manager of the Brislington House asylum from 1861 to 1894. Jake's sister, a scullery maid working at the house, died young and he himself had died soon after.

Sharon explained that for some unknown but presumably traumatic reason 'he couldn't get to the afterlife, so he spent years wandering about the building'.

Tradition relates that the executive's nocturnal visitation was so dramatic that he suffered a nervous breakdown and couldn't return to work. There may also have been other disturbances as a priest was called in to conduct an exorcism. Sharon told me that at the climax of the ritual 'Jake's sister came back and got him and that was the last anyone heard of him.'

Ever since then, apart from occasional high spirits at team-building events and theme parties, the house has been peaceful.

A number of other local premises suffered disturbances sufficient to warrant a plea for the intercession of the Church. In October 1992 the Reverend Stewart Jones (vicar of St Luke's from 1992 to 1997 when he became Assistant Chaplain

An exorcism has restored the peace of The Beeches, now a hotel

to the Archbishop of Canterbury) was called to assist a householder in Winchester Road. Details are scant for reasons of confidentiality, but the Rev. Jones had been asked to remove a negative presence from the home. He duly visited and performed a Holy Communion service to re-establish a peaceful atmosphere.

A similar service was performed by the Reverend Osmund Moss at a house in Hungerford Road in the 1960s.

St Luke's Church
Church Parade

The church and its tower have stood as a spiritual sentry over the village of Brislington for some six hundred years, and a chapel is thought to have existed on the same site at least a hundred years earlier still.

Although urban encroachment has robbed St Luke's of much of the grandeur and charm of its hillside location, echoes of its original rustic atmosphere can still be savoured in certain quiet spots in the ancient churchyard. The church seems a natural setting for supernatural stories, but we must remember that it is in spite of the teachings of the ministers that stories of ghosts persist within its walls.

The earliest spectral visitations relate to the Reverend Walker Mahoney Kirk, who became perpetual curate of St Luke's in his late twenties in 1885, a position he held for just eleven months.

He had lodgings along the Bath Road and his landlady heard the sound of a gunshot about an hour after midnight on the morning of Good Friday, April 23rd, 1886. When his body was discovered later that morning his hand was still clutching the six-chamber revolver with which he had shot himself – the bullet lodging in his brain.

The Coroner's Enquiry was held in the White Hart, Brislington Hill and reported in a local newspaper.[1] It revealed that the Rev. Kirk had been 'under the care' of Dr Fox of the Brislington House asylum. It was, however, the doctor's brother, Dr Bonville Fox, who was called to certify death, so he was called to give evidence to the inquest (Bonville Road is a tribute to him).

Dr Bonville Fox stated the deceased 'suffered from delusions and said he was being persecuted, and that Moses talked with him'. This comment is especially intriguing as the Passion of Easter is intimately associated with the slaughter of the Passover when Moses won permission to lead the Israelites out of Egypt. And it was in the middle of the night that the Angel of Death infamously claimed the lives of so many of Egypt's sons.[2]

He added, 'at night the deceased would walk about the neighbourhood trying, as he said, to get away from some horrible foes who were continually persecuting him.' The nature, or super-nature, of these 'horrible foes' remains open to conjecture.

The coroner directed the jury to interpret the suicide as temporary insanity, a verdict they endorsed, allowing the Rev. Kirk's body to be interred in the churchyard rather than consigned to un-consecrated ground, which was the rule with ordinary victims of suicide. Apparently though, despite the full rites of burial in a place of honour beside the west door, his spirit still could not find the peace he had so tragically sought and rumours of disturbances in the church began to spread. Sadly, with the passage of more than a century, the details of those incidents have been forgotten, persisting only in a deep-rooted tradition that the church was haunted, and the Rev. Kirk's unquiet ghost was responsible.

Another incident, which may have been related, was vivid enough to frighten a grown man out of the building. The late Bert Roach, who was born and bred in Brislington, told local historian and author Jonathan Rowe the story of

1. *Bristol Times and Mirror*, 27 April 1886.
2. *The Bible*, Exodus 11-12.

what happened to him one dark evening in the mid-1930s, when he was the Assistant Organist of St Luke's.

As a young man in his mid-twenties, Bert was alone in the church, practising at the organ in the organ chamber through the arch to the left of the chancel. Jonathan recalls: 'He heard heavy footsteps coming up behind him towards the chancel.' Bert looked around but there was nobody there. 'He heard them several times, getting nearer and nearer.' The footsteps actually climbed the steps and entered the chancel itself, but he couldn't see anybody there. When his nerves could stand it no longer, Bert 'got out as quickly as possible' as Jonathan phrased it.

Site of the old organ at St Luke's

Bert didn't know it at the time but 'under the tower there was a body in a coffin, a patient from Brislington House' (the same asylum attended by the Rev. Kirk). It has often been assumed that those ghostly footsteps emanated from that coffin, but it would be a very irreverent ghost that would walk right up into the chancel of a church, a curate would have done this routinely.

There is a popular idea amongst parapsychologists that physical objects can record extreme emotions – the Stone Tape theory. Could the Rev. Kirk's suicidal anxiety have generated mental energies powerful enough to imprint on the very stonework of the church? The theory suggests that a haunting occurs (e.g. the recording is replayed) when certain conditions somehow manage to stimulate and trigger playback. How such activation occurs varies from haunting to haunting, but this particular haunting features sound – the footsteps and the organ. Perhaps we are literally dealing with some sort of psychic echo.

In the context of the Stone Tape theory, it is notable that the organ chamber was built in 1883, only a couple of years before the Rev. Kirk took up office. As such, it would have been a practically blank canvas that could capture the full impact of his fight for sanity, a struggle that surely peaked in the days leading up to the commemoration of Jesus's own betrayal and death – Easter.

Sunset at Easter in 1936 would have been at 7pm, which would have given ample time for night to fall while Bert rehearsed (he was a working man with a day job). The church in general and the chancel in particular would have been dark, as described in his account of the haunting. Although it is improbable that Bert Roach would have been practising on Good Friday itself, perhaps he was rehearsing in preparation for the Christian calendar's holiest feast days, the self-same days in which the curate's troubled mind might have led him into the chancel, distraught, alone and at night, exactly fifty years before.

This would allow us to shine a ray of optimism into the gloom of the curate's darkest hours. Just as the 50th anniversary of his death may have triggered the church to replay its grim recording to Bert Roach, the unknown nineteenth century hauntings may also have been merely triggered recordings. Because this type of haunting does not indicate the presence of an earthbound soul, we could mercifully suppose that Walker Mahoney Kirk's spirit did indeed find in death the peace he failed to find in life.

St Luke's is a focal point in the spiritual battle that theologians have always envisioned as raging for the souls of their flock, so it is only natural that it is protected by a veritable arsenal of sacred symbols, including a company of fearsome gargoyles.

The most striking feature of the church's sacred architecture is its position in the landscape. It is carefully oriented so the congregation face towards the rising sun while they listen to the gospel, literally the 'good news'. Anyone who has endured a long, cold and uncomfortable night can appreciate the uplifting psychological impact of the dawn, and the religious symbolism is too obvious to have been unintentional. Likewise, graves are individually aligned so that their resident corpses may respond to the trump of Judgement Day and sit up facing the glory of the Risen Christ in the east.

Such alignments are not Christian innovations. We need only think of the nearby World Heritage Site of Stonehenge, with its famous alignment to the midsummer sunrise, to realise the antiquity of this natural allegory: the relevant phase of Stonehenge was constructed more than two millennia before Mary gave birth to a new religion. Similarly, the communal graves of Neolithic – New Stone Age – farmers were often painstakingly aligned so that their entrances faced the rising sun (numerous Neolithic flint tools have been found in Brislington). Newgrange, built before 3,300 BCE in the Boyne Valley, Eire, is the most famous example, in which a shaft of light from the mid-winter sunrise enters the great stone chamber at the core of the tomb. The penetration of the dark mound by the life-giving shaft of the sun suggests a sacred sexual metaphor in which a magical rekindling of life allows the tomb of the ancestors' spirits to become the womb of their rebirth. Certainly the hope of personal resurrection is still popularly celebrated in the seasonal festivals of the present-day religious calendar – most notably of course at Easter.

Such correspondences are common in religions employing astronomical symbolism; in fact they are so prevalent that an alien visitor could conclude that Earth's fundamental religion is a form of astrology.

Home
Where The Heart Is

Most of the ghosts whose stories fill these pages were complete strangers to the witnesses, but this does not give a true picture of hauntings. I believe most sightings involve ghosts who are well known to the witness – usually close

friends or relatives – but as these visits are often intensely personal, witnesses tend to shy away from any sort of publicity. So I am particularly grateful for the following contribution, which offers a glimpse into a wider but largely private world of common experience.

'My grandmother Lilian died in 1988 and I have seen her twice since. The first time was in 1992 just after my husband and I had bought our house, and before we even had any furniture in. It was a bright, sunny but cold afternoon and I was alone: she appeared in the living room, looked around smiling, nodding approvingly, then vanished again. Interestingly, she looked as she does in a photograph of her in her late twenties, not ninety as she was when she died.

'The second time was after we brought our son home from the maternity hospital in 1995. This time it was more a presence

Lillian, an approving grandmother and loving great grandmother than an actual image: I was alone again, sensed her leaning over my shoulder gazing at the baby in my arms, and felt her smile gently.'

Another sort of ghost story that is almost always neglected is that reported by children. Perhaps it is because some children lacking excitement in their lives hit upon ghosts as a topic they can revel in; certainly, exploring the dark and mysterious side of life adds interest to the dullest day. But I rather feel that a blanket disregard for the many and wonderful tales told by children would smother a potentially revealing section of the overall picture. On the other hand, we should perhaps not take them too seriously. After all, even adults frequently mistake something unusual for something paranormal, and children have a much smaller well of experience upon which to draw – a shortage naturally compensated for by a correspondingly deep fund of imagination. Every case is different and each deserves due respect.

Here is a story that stands out from the 'imaginary friend' genre. A nine-year-old boy was swinging at the end of their garden when he saw a 'grey man' walk into the house at the back door. It was around 5.30pm on August 2nd, 2004, a bright day during the summer holidays. The man wore a grey jacket and trousers that matched his grey hair; and the jacket had lots of pockets.

His parents were in the garden too and the child told them somebody had gone into the house. They instantly mounted a search but found no one and nothing was disturbed, not even the dog – who knew his job as guard dog and always performed his duty with great enthusiasm. Perhaps the parents were spooked by this inexplicable event, for they each separately saw 'something' out of the corner of the eye over the next month or two, something that could have been a grey man.

On a lighter note, on December 10th, 2002, younger children at a local junior school reported seeing Santa's sleigh flying through the swirling flurries of the first snow of the season.

It is a sad fact that most children are put-off talking about their little mysteries by parents who, rather than spend time discussing them, simply refuse to listen. But worse treatment can lie in store for adults who do not master the art of discretion.

On February 4th, 1833 a Commission of Inquiry sat at The Bear Inn, Devizes, Wiltshire, 'to enquire whether Sophia Frances Mary Caulfeild was a lunatic'.[1] She had been under the care of Doctor Fox of Brislington House, Bath Road since December 5th, 1832.

The preamble stated, 'The unfortunate subject of this inquiry is between 30

1. *Devizes and Wiltshire Gazette*, February 7th, 1833. Quotations are reproduced here with kind permission of Richard Heaton, and have been extracted from his transcript published at his website http://freepages.genealogy.rootsweb.com/~dutillieul/ZOtherPapers/D%26WGFebruary71833.html [accessed 23.06.05].

and 40 years of age, of the most refined and delicate manners, and of considerable intellectual powers and attainments. The origin of the disorder (mania) to which she has, no doubt, for a great length of time been subjected, has been traced to an excessive grief for the loss of an only sister, who died in 1817, and from which time the disorder has been rapidly increasing.'

Dr Francis Fox, son of the asylum's founder, was one of dozens of witnesses in attendance to give evidence of Miss Caulfeild's mental incapacity. He concluded his testimony: 'She refused to take medicine, and frequently attacked the person who attended her, and was so violent at one time, that it was necessary to put a strait waistcoat on her. It is very common for insane persons to hold conversation with spiritual beings, whom they imagine to be in the room. Miss Caulfeild has apparently been in conversation with a sister who died some years since, and has directed the servant to bring some bread and cheese for Satan. From the 5th of December to the 1st of January, and from the 11th of January to this time[1], I have never seen her in what I consider a state of complete mental soundness.'

Eventually, Miss Caulfeild had the opportunity to cross-examine the doctor. It began in earnest:

Dr F Fox (addressing her): I think you are a lunatic.

Miss Caulfeild: What are you reasons, Dr Fox ..?

Dr Fox: Is not your sister Emma dead, and have you not been speaking to her, as if she had been present?

Miss Caulfeild: I am glad you came to the facts. I had a sister Emma, it is true, but I trust she is in Heaven. Now, gentlemen, Doctor Francis Fox and his wife sleep in the next room to me, and it appears have overheard me talking of my sister Emma, which they have mistakenly construed into me talking to her. Surely such evidence as this will not convict me of a loss of my senses.

Whether we incline to believe her address to the gentlemen of the jury eloquently denying she spoke to her dead sister's spirit, or whether we trust the doctor's assertion under oath, the fact remains that the accusation was entered and accepted as evidence of her insanity. The jury, having heard much evidence besides, returned their verdict with little hesitation: Miss Caulfeild was of unsound mind.

Incidentally, Dr Francis Fox became a churchwarden of St Luke's in that same year, 1833; when he died in 1883, the clock in the church tower was erected in his memory.

---

1. He talked elsewhere of her 'paroxysm of mania, which commenced on the first and continued until the 11th of January'. He is saying here that even when not in the throes of complete mental breakdown, she was still unbalanced.

Nightingale Valley

This wooded valley was once owned by Wick House (formerly Newycke). The following two spooky sightings have been included despite the witness's own doubts about his interpretation as ghosts; at very least the tale serves to illustrate some important points.

One bright afternoon in late summer in or around 2000, he was on the footpath beside Brislington Brook from St Anne's Terrace, approaching the Packhorse Bridge.[1] From a distance of about 30 metres he glimpsed a person on the middle of the bridge. The figure appeared to be male, middle-aged, of average height and build, and wearing dark, brownish clothes.

The man seemed to be heading across the bridge towards him but trees hid him from sight for a moment (these trees have since been felled). When the man failed to reappear the witness couldn't imagine how he'd disappeared in such a short span of time. He remembers thinking, 'There has to be a natural explanation, but perhaps this is how some ghost stories start.'

The second incident occurred at 4.30pm on September 4th, 2003. The weather was, again, clement. The witness was descending southwards along the footpath from Allison Avenue and had nearly reached the flat wooded area around the weir. He noticed someone else had also just entered the patch of woodland from the main path through the water meadow (this path connects directly with the Packhorse Bridge), about 20 metres away.[2] The figure was a middle-aged male, of average height and build, and was wearing a dark brown suit. Seconds later, the man disappeared and, despite a search (the uncanny disappearance reminded the witness of the first incident), couldn't be found.

In neither incident did the man behave furtively, and there was little opportunity for him to conceal himself. It is simply these inexplicable disappearances that struck the witness as odd. He is familiar with Nightingale Valley in all seasons and for more years than he cares to remember.

It is tempting to suggest that these sightings could be simply the dark trunks of trees standing out from surrounding foliage, glimpsed through the corner of the eye. Indeed, this was the preferred view of the witness himself – until the second incident. But each time the light was good, the man was clearly visible, and he appeared perfectly solid.

On an historical note, it is worth observing that the Packhorse Bridge is the main hub of routes through Nightingale Valley, with footpaths radiating in six directions. Its foundations are medieval, and it is situated adjacent to a ford of stone blocks and large, cut timbers of uncertain date.

---

1. This bridge is located at ST 62127180 (all grid references relate to Ordnance Survey maps).
2. ST 62047165.

However, more recent building works may be more pertinent: a careful examination of the locations show that both sightings occurred when the witness was directly underneath the high voltage electricity cables that straddle this picturesque valley on woefully intrusive pylons. The effect of electromagnetism on the sensitive electric web of the human mind is currently a subject of heated research – some researchers recently discovered strong magnetic fields can stimulate the temporal lobes of the brain, triggering mild hallucinations in certain individuals. This susceptibility has also been linked with the erratic behaviour of animals before earthquakes, which can create a massive electrical charge as the quartz crystals in the earth's crust are deformed.

Knowing that the witness would like a rational explanation for his encounters with the paranormal, I am happy to propose the following theory: a powerful electromagnetic field strong enough to disorient a relaxed mind, combined with tree trunks suggestive of a human figure, triggered anomalous experiences.

On the other hand, perhaps it was just a ghost.

Wick House
191 Wick Road
Built in the late eighteenth century on the site of Newycke, thought to have been the home of the priests of St Anne's Chapel, this charming Georgian mansion is currently run by a housing association. But our touching little story is set shortly after the close of the Second World War, when it belonged to the Church of England Children's Society, originally known as the Waifs and Strays Society, which ran the house from 1925 to 1981.

Dorrie Brewer told me that she had been a live-in nurse at the house and, although she never experienced anything herself, she recalls that in 1948 or 1949 a girl said she had 'seen her mother on the landing'. This was the main, first-floor landing. Whether this was indeed a visitation from the spirit of the child's deceased mother, or merely a vain imagining, the meeting must have brought the girl a little comfort in a time of emotional crisis.

Another snippet of ghost lore involves a folly or summerhouse built in the fashion of a castle at Broomhill.[1] It was situated in the shrubbery of the extensive grounds of Wick House, and was partly covered with ivy of age great enough to allow boys to climb up onto the roof. It was said to be haunted but it seems at least as likely that the fertile imagination of youth mingled with the evocative architecture and lonely situation among the trees which – spiced with the thrill of being on forbidden territory – created an atmosphere of infectious

1. F C Jones & W G Chown 1977, *History of Bristol's Suburbs*, 129, Bristol, Reece Winstone. Based on the description in the book and examination of an 1886 Ordnance Survey map I have satisfied myself that this folly was located at ST 62337153 between Latimer Close and Alison Avenue.

otherworldliness.

Here, then, thoughts of ghosts, pirates, cavaliers, knights and damsels in distress might crowd together with impunity, uncensored by the strict routines of everyday life. Such a free and favoured spot may in fact be said to be inhabited by a true *genius loci*, or spirit of the place, inspiring visions of loveliness or doom.

Arnos Vale Cemetery
Bath Road

Inspired by the Georgian fashion for classical architecture, this rural valley was carefully transformed into a romantic vision of an ancient Greek necropolis. There is nothing even remotely tranquil however, about some of the ghosts reputed to haunt its wooded slopes.

The First World War (1914-18) created carnage and tragedy on an industrial scale, and hundreds of names are listed in the cemetery's memorial to the Great War. Amid such overwhelming loss of life, it is all too easy to forget the suffering of those who were left behind: one young woman who lost her love to the war machine also, it seems, lost her mind to grief and pined to her own untimely death.

Her spirit has been seen, clad in mourning black, weeping as she wanders among the graves. Her pitiable state is rendered all the more poignant as, it is said, she is fully aware of her situation. She has been known to appear to those whose hearts are troubled, and share with them what wisdom and guidance her short yet remarkable life can offer.

The circumstances that led to the second haunting are even more disturbing. Indeed, it is the stuff of nightmare: premature burial. The story goes that a distraught family whose daughter had submitted to illness mistakenly believed her to have slipped quietly away into God's care. Her body was duly committed to the grave. In fact, she had merely sunk into the deepest reaches of coma, and entered that profound death-like state known as catalepsy.

Upon awaking in the lightless confines of her tomb the agonising realisation dawned and, in the extreme emotion of her appalling plight, her spirit left her body to flee shrieking through the cemetery where it has been seen and heard wailing inconsolably.

The family were driven to exhume her body and took what comfort they could from the evidence that, given the frailty of her infirmity, she had instantly suffered a fatal shock that mercifully prevented a maddeningly slow descent into oblivion.

Richard Smith, current chairman of the Friends of Arnos Vale Cemetery, could not shed any light on these two tales, and suggested instead that the only nocturnal disturbances in the cemetery were relatively prosaic: vandalism.

Having been unable to interview any witnesses to these phenomena, I present them as anecdotes. I found them in a gazetteer of ghosts at The Shadowlands website.[1] The list includes general retellings of some famous stories, some well-reported personal experiences, and some rather dubious accounts that seem more like urban legends than conventional ghost stories.

Another sorrowing spirit has been described to me by Gary Milward (see the Arnos Manor Hotel) as an 'old man, sitting down, crying, with a cloth cap on'. Although Gary heard the story second-hand, he is in no doubt that it was reported in good faith.

I must confess that the highly sensational elements of the first two stories made me very suspicious of their authenticity; I even wondered whether or not to include them in this anthology. After all, if they had been 'made up' to scare people, then they are just as disruptive to the quiet charm of Arnos Vale as the vandals who occasionally desecrate the monuments themselves. However, there is at least one plausible explanation for them. As Richard Smith pointed out, there seems to be a perennial crop of thrill-seeking adolescents who, in the absence of other local entertainment, use (or, more properly, abuse) the cemetery as a spooky theme park and trysting place.

Under those conditions, it is easy to see how the nocturnal shrieks of hedgehogs, wails of courting cats, the furtive rustling of rats in the undergrowth, even the flitting shadows of owls under the moon, could all contribute to a scenario that an impressionable youngster could naively believe has supernatural rather than natural causes. It is notoriously easy for a suggestible mind to succumb to a creepy mood and confuse a few wild ideas of its own, for psychic communion with the spirit world. It's actually amazing that there aren't more stories of bizarre goings on in this spectacularly atmospheric place.

As well as the particular tragedies recalled in these tales, there is an altogether more heartening husband/wife relationship celebrated in a once popular but now secluded spot in the heart of the Vale. Theirs was a love that triumphed over religious division.

When the cemetery was opened in 1839, it accommodated both Church of England and other Christian denominations, but the two groups were rigorously segregated. This presented a powerful dilemma to Thomas and Mary Matthews, for he kept the Anglican faith while she was a Congregationalist: it

1. Shadowlord 1998 - 2005, www.theshadowlands.net/places/uk.htm [accessed 14.06.05].

The tomb of Thomas Matthews and his wife Mary at Arnos Vale Cemetery

seemed that a point of law was going to separate a couple whose marriage was meant to abide for eternity.

Fortunately, the family was possessed of considerable wealth and influence, and an ingenious solution was found. They bought burial plots on either side of a path that separated the Anglican from the Non-conformist sections; and then they bought the path itself.

When Thomas died in 1860, the two plots and part of the path were enclosed as a single area,[1] and he was laid to rest in the side consecrated according to Anglican rite. When Mary followed him in 1864, she was interred beside him with the services of her own faith. The impressive memorial stands testimony to the strength of their marital union, and a signal victory for religious tolerance.

36   1. ST 60727145.

Arnos Manor Hotel
470 Bath Road

Following a £2.5 million refurbishment in the early years of the twenty-first century, this remarkable complex has rediscovered an elegance and grandeur which had been eclipsed by several decades of use as a nightclub. Eccentric industrialist William Reeve built the original mansion in the 1760s, a bold development that included The Black Castle. New owners Forestdale Hotels carried out the repair work with close attention to the original character of the property ensuring a restoration sympathetic to the eighteenth century, but the ghost that once roamed this building does not seem to have been lured back by this return to the more genteel pace of a former age. Indeed, the ghost emanates from a later date, no earlier than the 1850s, when the site was donated to the Order of the Good Shepherd, and became a Roman Catholic convent.

The Order still exists and is, as it was, cloistered, with its nuns not only adopting the three ordinary vows (poverty, chastity, and obedience) but also committing themselves to work for the conversion and instruction of penitents. This particular convent suffered bomb damage during the air raids of 1941, and Brislington's nuns moved away shortly afterwards. Inevitably, Forestdale's renovation has not been without its compromises: the nun's cloister, for instance, is now a restaurant, and their chapel is a lounge.

Following a lead from an article in a local leaflet[1], I met Ted Sutor in 2003. He was a surveyor and a founder member of the Arno's Court County Club, which opened after extensive renovation in 1960. He had heard all the details about the ghostly nun from his wife Monica, now sadly deceased. Although Monica did not mention anything supernatural happening to herself, she had an uncanny knack of meeting people who had encountered or at least knew of the ghost. For instance, long after the heyday of the club in the Swinging Sixties, she fell into conversation with a couple of visiting nuns seated in Arnos Court Park (which, incidentally, had been farmland belonging to the convent). It turned out that they had both lived at the convent before the Second World War, and confirmed that the ghostly nun was well known among the sisters. One of the visitors was the Reverend Mother, and she added that the spirit was 'quite harmless, and wouldn't do harm to anybody'.

One of the first people at the club to see the ghostly nun, affectionately dubbed 'Sister Theresa', was Mrs Connie Hoyle, wife of a co-owner of the club. She saw the figure of a woman robed in a grey habit, ascending a staircase that had not yet been opened for use. The fact that the staircase was closed to the

---

1. 'When Stars Shone at Arno's Court', *The Brislington Bugle*, 17, Summer 1992, Bristol, Brislington Conservation and Amenity Society.

Arnos Manor Hotel

public suggested to Ted that the sighting must have been shortly before the grand opening, which was just in time for the Christmas festivities. The stairway involved was, apparently, the original Georgian flight rising from the reception area at the main entrance. The main entrance is unmistakable, and is located in the castellated building described by Horace Walpole in October 1766 as 'a smart false Gothic house'. The plainer adjoining wings are Victorian additions.

In the 1960s part of the Arno's Court complex was being used as a hotel and Monica Sutor heard that a guest had seen the nun gliding along a corridor. Ted believes the corridor to have been the one making a T-junction with the haunted stairs, on the first floor.

I also spoke with another founder member of the County Club, Betty Hutchings, who confirmed that the building was widely known to be haunted. She also told me of her own eerie experience in or around 1968. At that time it was a custom that, each Yuletide, the members arranged entertainment for the staff, which included not only preparing a meal and waiting on the tables, but clearing up afterwards (a custom wonderfully reminiscent of the social inversion that accompanied the midwinter Roman rites of Saturnalia).

While the staff were partying, Betty was working alone for a while in one of the kitchen rooms loading dirty crockery onto a conveyor belt feeding into an industrial dish washer that was about two metres long. It was late evening, around 11 o'clock.

'I was on my own,' she said, 'standing at the washing machine, when I felt something on my right. I looked and nobody was there. It was as if someone had gone behind my back. I looked to my left and I saw the swing door open and go away from me, and come back closed. It was a bit weird and I felt frightened.'

Despite the shock, she stayed in the room and, demonstrating considerable nobility of character, completed her duties. I am very grateful to Betty for this first-hand account, not least because as it allows me to observe that the Chinese Whispers effect is a significant obstacle to any careful researcher. I had previously heard her story from someone who heard it from somebody else – but in that version the ghost had actually materialised, and it was the nun herself, dressed in a white robe, who walked through the room!

Betty Britton, who worked at the club in the late 1960s and 70s told me, 'one Sunday I was asked to take a cup of tea to someone in the hotel. I had to go downstairs and walked along where the nuns' bedrooms were. It was cold and a bit chilly, and the hairs on the back of my neck were standing up. I had heard about the ghost of the nun. I wouldn't go down there again.'

A similar story[1] is told by a man who worked there in 1977. Around 3am one August night he was rolling an empty keg along a stone-floored corridor that stretched almost the full width of the building, front to back. About mid-way was a wide wooden door and, as he passed through, a soft, feminine voice called his name. He span around to see who was there but the corridor, which ran for six or seven metres to the nearest corner, was deserted and silent. There were no doorways or alcoves to hide anyone, and he even checked for ventilation grills but could find no explanation for the mystery voice.

Later he learned that the voice had often been heard at the same spot; and then he was told the story of the nun's ghost. The legend centred on a nun who had killed herself: rather than burying her body in unconsecrated ground the decision was taken to immure her in the convent. Workmen discovered the disarticulated bones among the wreckage after the 1941 bombing but, with lamentable haste, discarded them with the rest of the debris. That's when the haunting began: even the night watchman became too terrified to stay at his post.

Other incidents he heard about during his employment in 1977 included sightings of a woman dressed in brown whose reflection was glimpsed but the

---

1. Retold here with thanks to Darren Mann, webmaster of www.paranormaldatabase.com, for sharing details of correspondence submitted to his website.

person was never there, and doors that refused to stay locked.

In 1996 the premises were known as the Parkside Hotel, and Sue Le'Queux relates that the new manager John Bird discovered a wide variety of supernatural goings-on, including not only nuns and figures in grey habits, but an old man in a tweed suit, clearly seen in a bar-room mirror; a maid wearing an old-fashioned uniform who walked straight through a wall; and even minor poltergeist phenomena such as a rattling door and toiletries tossed around.[1]

In 2003 I met Gary Milward (Sales Manager for the newly named Arnos Manor Hotel), and he referred to the persistent rumour that the ghost was that of a 'pregnant nun who was walled up alive', saying that although he had made thorough enquiries about her, he had failed to find any employee who had actually witnessed anything in the least bit spooky.

The fact that the convent operated a reformatory school for girls (up to 200 of them, and it was the first such Roman Catholic establishment in England), suggests a connection with wayward young women, but the idea of immuring Sister Theresa for sexual misconduct seems an absurd horror story exploiting a caricature of medieval Christian barbarity – in short, an urban myth. It is much more likely that the original story celebrated a kind-hearted nun whose death was deeply mourned, and whose comforting presence remained in the hearts and minds of the sisters as a sort of spiritual guardian, eventually becoming somehow woven into the fabric of the closed, cloistered convent itself.

Gary Milward also mentioned the tradition of there being three tunnels radiating from the old building. One allegedly leads towards Crew's Hole where William Reeve had his profitable smelting works. A second secret passageway apparently ran to Arnos Vale Cemetery (for what purpose is unclear), and the third, which is well documented, gave subterranean access to The Black Castle.

The Black Castle
St Philips Causeway
This public house is probably the single most photographed building in Brislington, and its architecture, atmosphere, and ghosts are certainly remarkable. In fact, to celebrate the importance of this site as a centre of supernatural activity, I sent some information to Sue Le'Queux for her book in 2004.[2] Without repeating those details unnecessarily, it is worth reiterating that my contribution concerned two ghosts: one was a little girl who was seen recently in the ladies' toilets, but who vanished without trace. The other spirit is altogether more complex and challenging.

1. Sue Le'Queux 2004, *Haunted Bristol*, 58, Stroud, Tempus.
2. *Ibid.* The illustration labelled 'The Black Castle' on page 60 is actually the Arnos Manor Hotel.

The Black Castle, or Arno's Castle as it used to be known, started life in the 1760s as a stable-block, brewery, laundry and servants' quarters belonging to the mansion built by William Reeve, now known as Arnos Manor Hotel. Its strikingly iridescent black stonework is actually composed of blocks of slag cast at Reeve's brass foundry.

It also has a chapel at the top of its largest tower and, if a large (3 metres x 3 metres) red sign prominently displayed outside the pub in the 1980s is anything to go by, The Black Castle was proud of its reputation of being 'haunted by a ghost which lives in the original chapel above the bar.'

Without wishing to read too much into what might have been merely a witty turn of phrase, the fact that the sign says the ghost 'lives' in the chapel may be significant. The chapel certainly came to be regarded as the focus for a very vigorous haunting indeed.

In 1992 assistant managers Teresa and Bruce Boorer told me of the tradition that a nun haunts the building, but they had seen nothing more than weird shadows. And the following year new managers Karen and Trevor Kane told me how they had been plagued by doors that refused to stay shut – even if they had been locked and alarmed, this is a theme to which we shall return.

My wife Joules and I were invited to tour the building on the afternoon of December 30th, 1993, and we were able to visit and photograph the chapel – a privilege Karen did not offer lightly as she had learned to her cost that the disturbances rapidly followed when somebody had been 'disrespectful' about the nun. I am happy to say our visit occasioned no reports of unrest.

At around 1am on that night however, a bizarre event occurred while Karen was chatting with her husband and several members of staff in what was then the Jester's Bar. The subject of our visit to the chapel cropped up and, inevitably, conversation turned to the nun. Just then the illuminated 'EXIT' sign above a door abruptly flashed on and off several times. Karen, who had developed a

The Black Castle

The chapel at The Black Castle

sort of sympathy for the spirit, understood that the nun was bidding her a fond farewell – their tenancy was about to end as the pub was closing for extensive refurbishment.

One member of staff reported that she had seen 'headless nuns' in the restaurant in the mid-1990s. Although this particular incident immediately reminded me of the more doubtful elements of Arnos Vale Cemetery hauntings, it would be wrong to dismiss it outright. The choir sisters at the convent across the road (now Arnos Manor Hotel) wore a white habit and scapular, with a black veil. In a dark room, the ghost of such a nun might indeed appear to have no face.

In 2003 I spoke with assistant manager Miss Louise Noon who told me that around 1am one day in in August 2002 some glasses had inexplicably flown off a shelf and smashed in front of several witnesses. She singled out the restaurant as being particularly haunted: strange chills were often felt there, and small items such as cutlery and pens frequently disappeared, often mere moments after being put down. Her cat Tommy, who roamed freely, refused to enter the restaurant.

Unfortunately, Tommy's apparent psychic sensitivity, coupled with a cat's innate curiosity, may have aroused enmity from the spirit world. If so, he was not the first to suffer. Louise told me that people had noticed previous managers' cats had 'gone missing or were knocked over'. Louise was told in no uncertain terms: 'Get rid of the cat'.

'Everybody warned me when I came here,' Louise recalled. Sadly, the foretold tragedy came true, and Tommy (who was fairly streetwise and had survived other hazardous environs), was knocked down on the main road that runs beside the pub. 'I did tell you,' was the stark comment from one regular after the fatal accident.

Could all this animosity be associated with the Church's old hatred of cats – regarding them as familiar spirits and agents of the Devil? We may note in passing that cats were cruelly persecuted by the Christian establishment as scape-goats during the Black Death. Ironically, those very cats were one of humanity's few allies at that time, as they would have preyed on the rats whose fleas carried the plague.

Against this, the Black Castle is rather isolated. There is no network of garden fences to explore, and no patchwork of gardens to enjoy. Surrounded by traffic, it is easy to imagine a wholly mundane reason for the pub's reputed unfriendliness to resident felines.

Following publication of *Haunted Bristol*, another ex-manager has contacted me about his own experiences, which included the door of his bedroom, which was situated above the old stables, opening of its own accord.

At first he assumed he hadn't closed it properly and a draught was simply moving it, but on one occasion he actually watched as the door handle moved downwards. He was alone in the building at the time and believed he was about to be confronted by a burglar – with admirable fortitude he raced across the room and tugged the door open to catch the intruder off-guard. But nobody was there.

Several other times he had been in the room when he heard the sound of footsteps approaching along the corridor outside. Again, when he checked to see if it was one of the staff, the apartment was empty.

He also told me about mysterious shadows that moved across the courtyard when the pub was closed. He and other witnesses had searched in vain to find any possible cause for these seemingly common yet unfathomable phenomena.

It is notable that he took pains to say that although he was familiar with the tradition of the nun, he couldn't definitely link his own experiences with her. And if there is a snag in the coherent accounts of the Black Castle's ghostly nun, it is that there is no record whatsoever that any nun lived anywhere on the premises, ever. But what of the tunnel that had connected The Black Castle with Arnos Manor Hotel (which saw service as a convent)? Couldn't that have provided the link? Unfortunately, long before any nuns arrived at the Arnos Manor Hotel portion of the original estate, the Black Castle part had been sold separately, and the access tunnel under the A4 Bath Road had been sealed.

What can we make of this bizarre twist in the tale? We are, it seems, left standing – eyes drifting heavenwards, mouth agape. If so, we'd be the living image of the façade of the chapel tower.

In fact, the architectural conceit of forming a face sculpted in mullioned windows and an ornamental arch, gives us a remarkable clue. As we enter the

The face of the facade at
The Black Castle tower

courtyard from the main entrance, this mighty visage completely dominates us
– even if only noticed subliminally, such a literally towering presence can stir
our subconscious and profoundly affect our mood.

To cross the threshold of that tower, ascend, and enter the space within that
gigantic head – the chapel itself – and gaze out through its unblinking eyes,
invites us to view the world from a truly mind-altering perspective. Peering out
through those giant yet benign eyes – the windows of the soul – we can glimpse
a world not measured in mortal time but in the creeping duration of stone. We
sense the immeasurable stillness that has witnessed the passage of centuries
and the procession of generations.

Such a spot would certainly deserve a strong reputation as a sacred place. In
such a site we can see beyond our mundane selves, and apprehend a larger
truth; we may readily envision a reality that belongs to the immortal spirit.

Apparently, William Reeve's indulgence in architectural oddity and his fascination for monumental antiquities placed a great burden on his finances and, in
1774, he was declared bankrupt. Rather than rallying to the support of a fallen
fellow, the Society of Friends expelled him from their company. Although Reeve
was plainly somewhat eccentric, the precise nature of his religious misconduct

is unclear, but such a sanction is used only after extreme measures have failed to bring a wayward soul back into accord with deepest Quaker principals.

Incidentally, the Black Castle was once dubbed 'The Devil's Cathedral' – this inspired name was coined by that English man of letters Horace Walpole (1717–1797) when he saw it in 1766. He certainly appreciated its style: his own residence, Strawberry Hill, near Twickenham, was a gothicized pseudo-castle that has been acclaimed as the finest early gothic revival building in Britain (his infectious enthusiasm actually helped undermine the Georgian obsession for classical and Italianate design).

Walpole may also have relished its reputation for ghostly phenomena; his supernatural romance *The Castle of Otranto* was published in 1764, and started a fashion for the genre.

To end on a lighter note, I am certain that the latest notion about the Devil's Cathedral – that a buck-toothed vampire has been seen atop the tallest tower, baring its fangs to the heavens – is not a significant part of the ancient tradition. We should, I am sure, dismiss it as if it were a grinning gargoyle teasing us with nonsense.

The Woodlands
94 – 96 West Town Lane
This early eighteenth-century building was split into two homes in 1938, but the origin of the haunting evidently predates this division as it involves the ghosts of a horse and rider (reputedly a man) that approached right up to what was then the front door.[1] I am grateful to Kenneth Ingham, who has lived in the house since the 1960s, for informing me that he has heard nothing of this haunting in all that time.

The Elms
Bonville Road
The Elms, a once elegant Georgian mansion, parts of which dated from the seventeenth century, was demolished after a fire in 1938. According to Frederick Jones, apparently writing in the early 1940s,[2] the route of the Bath road used to lie further to the north than the modern A4, and ran through open fields between Long Fox Manor and the Avon. This is important because part of the old road was used as the drive to The Elms; and this driveway was haunted by a phantom carriage drawn by four ghostly horses, that drove down to the house.

---

1. Jonathan Rowe and Diddie Williams 1986, *Bygone Brislington*, 12, privately printed.
2. Frederick C Jones undated, *History of Brislington and St Annes*, 27, privately printed. This volume appears to consist of typewritten copies of newspaper articles appearing in the *Bristol Evening Post*; the date of this story being March 20, 1941 (the edition of this date held on microfilm at the Bristol Reference Library does not contain the article).

The Ordnance Survey map of 1886 shows the only drive to The Elms was Blind Lane (now partly incorporated into Bonville Road, meeting the A4 as a mere footpath). However, despite a complex network of tracks and paths crossing what was then a patchwork of fields, this drive appears to be a dead end and does not continue northwards to intersect with an older arterial route between Bristol and Bath. We can only surmise that the main road had already fallen into disuse and been lost by that time.

One possible route for the earlier road is today a public right of way heading southeast from Ironmould Lane across open fields towards Keynsham. From the gate this footpath points straight towards the site of Keynsham Abbey and also towards the present day church of St John with its prominent tower, and may have connected it with the medieval Chapel of St Anne's in the Wood, which was part of the old parish of Keynsham and administered by the Abbey.

This medieval road might have followed the even more ancient line of the Roman road that is believed to have connected Brislington Villa with Keynsham Villa – if so, its alignment suggests the Romans either forded the Avon at St Anne's or used a ferry which is believed to have operated there in the medieval period. Such old, straight tracks may also be evaluated as ley lines, but this route has insufficient antiquities acting as markers to qualify it as a plausible ley.

Brislington Hall
Brislington Retail Park

Another old building that has disappeared is Brislington Hall, which was built around 1770 and demolished in 1933; a superstore now occupies part of its site although much of the mansion itself lies under the car park in front of the store.

The Hall was home to some of the most influential people in the area: its founder was James Ireland, the High Sheriff of Somerset. He married Frances Godde, one of the country's most wealthy heiresses, and became the largest landowner in Brislington. Some fifteen years after his death the Queen of Portugal came to visit in 1828 when she heard about the magnificent blossoming of one of his plants, an aloe almost 60 years old that had produced a spectacular flower spike some 7.5 metres tall. At one time a flock of peacocks roamed the gardens.

It was during the tenure of the last Squire of Brislington, Alfred Clayfield-Ireland, that a parlour maid reported some unusual events. She worked at the Hall around 1920, and once when she was in the ballroom that had witnessed the gaiety of high society, she plainly heard a clock chiming 6pm – yet there was no clock in the room. On another occasion at Brislington Hall she saw a man attired in evening dress disappear in front of her eyes.

St Anne's Well
St Anne's Wood

There is a ghost associated with this ancient well but, although it is known to have haunted the immediate vicinity of the holy spring, the details of what it looks like (or even if it is visible at all) are unknown.

The ghost is mentioned in a book of regional scope that presents a wealth of information relating to the history of St Anne's Well.[1] The well is set amidst railings at the edge of a narrow flood plain in the steep-sided wooded valley through which Brislington Brook has meandered for thousands of years. In 1790, Rev. Collinson described the scene: 'A more retired spot could hardly be found. A deep well, overhung with aged oaks, alders, and poplars ... through it runs a languid brook, gently murmuring over a rocky bottom and making several waterfalls.'[2] This picturesque little gorge still survives, and actually has several other small springs along its eastern flank as it extends southwards into Nightingale Valley (its tranquillity, though, is today rather spoiled by the main Bristol to London railway line, which bisects it).

St Anne's Well has an illustrious history – even reigning monarchs were motivated to visit this humble water source – and it is also a cornucopia of folklore. In its heyday St Anne's Well rivalled both Canterbury, the seat of Christianity in England, and the Shrine of Our Lady of Walsingham, Norfolk (which, according to legend, had been miraculously built as a replica of the house where the divine messenger Gabriel announced the birth of Jesus). The reputation of this holy well was prodigious indeed.

Its nearby thirteenth-century Chapel was also a sizeable structure, reflecting its importance and wealth. It was solidly buttressed and some 17.5 metres in length. However, some claims that its roof was 24 metres high must stretch credulity beyond reasonable bounds.

The fame of this holy well arose from its reputed healing powers: its charmed waters were a particular source of comfort and aid for women desiring to conceive, as well as offering relief to anyone suffering from weak eyes or rheumatism. The latter claim may be the most easily explained because the white willow (Salix alba) thrives in such damp conditions, and a tea made of its bark boiled in well water would produce almost instant relief from a wide range of aches and pains. The other traditions though, are more thought-provoking.

---

1. Phil Quinn 1999, *Holy Wells of Bath & Bristol Region*, 149, Woonton, Logaston Press.
2. Rev A Richardson 1898, St Anne's Chapel, Brislington, *Proceedings of the Somersetshire Archaeological & Natural History Society*, XLIV, 197.

The sight of spring water gushing from a cleft in the ground reminds some of a key event that signals the culmination of pregnancy, when a woman's waters break in readiness for the delivery of her baby. Others regard the refreshing liquid as nature's own breast milk. Both points of view share a connection with childbirth and motherhood, and this well is most famous for its powers of relieving gynaecological problems. Its attribution to St Anne is very revealing in this respect.

The name Anne derives from the Hebrew feminine name Hannah, which translates as 'He [i.e. Yahweh, God] has favoured me [with a child]', borne in the Bible by a woman who triumphed over infertility.[1] However, St Anne was the centre of her own widespread and influential medieval cult that believed her to be the mother of the Virgin Mary.[2]

St Anne's role as the grandmother of Christ seems to have struck a chord with the medieval mind: her advanced age did not imply dementia but the exact opposite – razor sharp acuity and wisdom honed by a long lifetime's experience. She could be relied upon to know everything there is to know about 'women's problems' and St Anne had the ear of the Mother of God into the bargain.

In 1880 a couple of silver coins were found during an excavation of St Anne's Well: one was from the reign of Edward IV while the other was of Henry VII. By a bizarre stroke of fortune, these two kings feature in one of the most dramatic historical events associated with St Anne's Well.

Edward IV's eldest daughter, blonde-haired Elizabeth of York (traditionally regarded as the model for the Queen of Hearts on the English deck of playing cards), became the bride of Henry VII. Henry had established peace in the land following the end of the protracted Wars of the Roses, and was the first Tudor king. He was also a Welshman and his aspiration for a new dynasty founded on the pursuit of true justice and the ideals of chivalry, was enshrined in the naming of his first child Arthur in honour of the famous hero King Arthur.

At Whisuntide 1486, when Elizabeth was already pregnant with Arthur, Henry visited St Anne's Well. The antiquary John Leland quoted a succinct earlier document saying 'On the morne when the King had dyned he roode on pilgrimage to Sainte Anne's in the Woode.'[3] The timing of Henry's visit to the well is notable: Whitsuntide (also known as Pentecost) was a key date in the Arthurian calendar. It was, for instance, on this date that Arthur pulled the sword from the stone and anvil, thereby becoming king of England.[4] Prince Arthur was born on September 20th at Winchester, then believed to be built on the ruins of the legendary capital Camelot (such matters were not left to chance).

48
1. I Samuel, 1.
2. A belief not founded on any Biblical text but on the early apocryphal *Protevangelium of James*.
3. *Coll. De Rebus*, iv, 185.
4. Sir Thomas Malory, *Le Morte D'Arthur*, I, VII-VIII.

What the reign of this new King Arthur might have been like is anybody's guess, because Prince Arthur died on April 2nd, 1502. In the wake of his death Elizabeth became pregnant with her seventh child and, several months later on August 22nd, she herself made the pilgrimage to St Anne's Well. She donated a modest financial offering of two shillings and sixpence to the well's ecclesiastic guardians, as her Privy Purse Expenses reveal: 'for the Quenes offring to Saint Anne in the wood besides Bristowe ij s. vj d.'

Naturally, she would have been keenly concerned for a safe pregnancy and, like her husband 17 years earlier, would no doubt have sought St Anne's protective influence to oversee the birth of her child. Sadly though, just nine days after baby Katherine was born, Elizabeth died on February 11th, 1503, her 37th birthday. Katherine herself only survived her by about a week.

In 1508 a Welsh minstrel or 'harper' playing at St Anne's so moved his audience with, perhaps, inspiring ballads of Arthurian chivalry or a lament for dashed hope, that on June 22nd he received one shilling from the Duke of Buckingham. At that time, a shilling was a day's wage for a working man, making the Duke's donation a rough equivalent to tossing a modern busker several £20 notes.

The following year Henry VII died and his son, who ascended to the throne as King Henry VIII, sealed the doom of the chapel that had served St Anne's Well and its pilgrims for nearly 250 years. The infamous Dissolution of the Monasteries obliged the abbot and canons of Keynsham to surrender their lands to the king in January 1539, lands that included the holy well and Chapel of St Anne's in the Wood.

As the entire Roman Catholic institution of pilgrimage fell into disrepute as being 'superstitious', the Chapel fell into ruin, and St Anne's Well relinquished its official Christian patronage. It was still cherished by the local community, however, and through the centuries there have been numerous cycles of revival and lapse. In the early 1880s, landowner James Sinnott caused public outrage when he blocked public right of way to the site. A legal battle commenced, including testimony from witnesses who collected water from the well, which culminated in his defeat in 1891. In 1923 the Sinnott family sold the valley to the City and the following year historian Frederick C Jones (1892-1964) successfully campaigned for an annual public procession to the well on St Anne's Day – July 26th.

In 1996 there was even a serious attempt by a group of self-confessed pagans (The Source: Bristol Springs & Wells Group) to honour the spirit of the sacred well by a sympathetic restoration project.[1] Their renovation included stepping

1. Annie Wildwood 1995, www.bath.ac.uk/lispring/sourcearchive/ns4/ns4aw1.htm [accessed 22.06.05].

stones and a carved stone statue of St Anne, but this and the rest of the site became a target for vandalism, and little now remains.

The founder members of The Source were inspired by Janet and Colin Bord[1] to wonder whether the well's dedication to St Anne might conceal the pre-Christian name of the pagan deity Santan, which they translated as meaning 'Holy Fire'. This supposed association with light reminds us of the well's renown for curing eye problems; and its epithet 'holy' suggests the eye's spiritual equivalent: clairvoyance 'clear seeing' (we have already noted St Anne's incisive insight).

The idea that holy wells can heal eye complaints is surprisingly common. Perhaps the mirror-like surface of the water resembles our own pupils. In the case of St Anne's Well there is also a possible connection with the Teutonic god Odin (Anglo Saxon 'Woden' from whose name we derive Wednesday – Woden's Day).

Odin hankered after the second-sight of occult (literally 'hidden') knowledge, and he determined to drink from a well of wisdom whose waters nourished the middle root of the World-Tree Yggdrasil. But, to do this, he had to pluck out one of his eyes and give it to the well's guardian Mimir ('He who Thinks'). Only then did Odin achieve wisdom and inspiration (the holy fire that enlightens the mind).

It may seem fanciful to suppose a link between St Anne's Well and the pagan deity Woden, but we should remember that the waters from this spring were flowing for millennia before it was given a Christian name. There is also some circumstantial evidence to support the Anglo-Saxon connection. For instance the similarity of sound between Anne and Wan, another form of Woden, caught the attention of late nineteenth century and early twentieth century scholars such as R C Skyring Walters.[2] Moreover, the massive Wansdyke earthwork, literally 'Wan's / Woden's Dyke', is about seven kilometres from the well, which argues a strong presence for his cult in this area. In fact, the source of Brislington Brook, which runs beside St Anne's Well, can be traced to within 200 metres of Maes Knoll fort, where the Wansdyke begins on Dundry Hill. Even the name Brislington is Anglo-Saxon in origin and means, apparently, 'Beorhthelm's Farmstead'.

The idea of offering a sacrifice to the waters of a sacred spring has survived in the common habit of casting coins into a wishing well, and bronze and silver coins are still occasionally to be seen gleaming through the water of St Anne's Well.

The Celts are also renowned for their veneration of wells and springs, and

50   1. Janet and Colin Bord 1972, *Mysterious Britain*, 111, London, Garnstone Press.
2. RCS Walters 1928, *The Ancient Wells, Springs, and Holy Wells of Gloucestershire*, 65, Bristol, St Stephen's Press.

cherished the idea that such pools are entrances to the underworld. According to Evelyn Winchester[1] an earlier name for Brislington Brook was the Froome, a common Celtic river name derived from a word meaning 'Fair' or 'Brisk' (which may have been an apt description before much of the stream was diverted into a culvert). The traditions that still revolve around St Anne's Well are typical of ancient Celtic beliefs still current in other parts of Britain and Europe; beliefs that have their roots in an indigenous pantheism thriving long before Anne – or even Hannah herself – was born.

St Anne's Well in 1991

---

1. Evelyn Winchester 1986, *St Anne's Bristol, A History*, 8, Bristol, White Tree Books.

Mysteries

Brislington (Roman) Villa
Winchester Road

To look at it, nobody would guess that a section of Winchester Road[1] straddles the site of a Roman villa, complete with its own suite of heated baths. Brislington Villa was not a military camp, so we shouldn't imagine phantom legions tramping along the road. Instead, we could envisage a spacious, south-facing bungalow nearly 40 metres long, the home of a wealthy family.

The family, possibly local folk who had embraced the Roman way of life, may have derived their fortune from administering the area on behalf of Rome. Over the years, their success allowed them to add some extensions to their home; this and the quality of the mosaics that graced their floors indicate the family enjoyed a relatively luxurious lifestyle in the middle of the high-income bracket.

The villa was built around 270 CE, some fifty years before the Emperor Constantine adopted Christianity as the state religion (the progenitor of modern Roman Catholicism). Some tantalising clues as to the religious life of these sophisticated pagans are revealed in the mosaic floors.

A room to the east of the triclinium, the villa's equivalent of the dining room where guests were entertained, had a mosaic some three metres square and central to the colourful design is an elegant two-handled goblet for wine, a cantharus. At the corners of this square panel are four 'lotus' flowers, a traditional motif that appears both elsewhere in this mosaic and in the triclinium itself. This combination of wine and lotus flowers is a hallmark of certain Mystery Religions tracing their origins to ancient Egypt.

Many Mystery cults were flourishing throughout the Roman world at that time. Devotees of Bacchus and Dionysus are famous for using wine to induce a bodily intoxication that was taken as symbolic of the divine liberation enjoyed by their highest initiates.

The lotus flower, the emblem of Upper (Southern) Egypt, is actually the blue water-lily, a wonderfully scented blossom with bright blue petals arrayed around a golden centre. The flower closes its petals each night, sometimes even sinking below the surface of the water, and re-emerging in the morning in all its beauty. It does not take much imagination to see a clear parallel with the sun's journey beneath the horizon each night, and its glorious resurrection the next morning. And it is only one more step to see this striking imagery as a metaphor for the soul: once submerged in spiritual darkness, now awakening into illumination, the dead being made alive.

---

1. ST 61657093.

Inner transformation is the essence of the teachings of the true Mystery Schools.[1] A student achieving initiation into such a mystery would have a deeply moving experience that may be likened to awakening after a long and intense dream. A hallmark of their new and enhanced consciousness would be a feeling of strength which, tempered by the School's wholesome lessons, would be vivified by a profound sense of their own innate personal authority. As such, it is no accident that the 'lotus' motif appears on ancient sceptres of kingship.

Incidentally, its ancient associations with royalty continue into the present day. The fleur-de-lys, although nominally identified as the Yellow Flag (Iris pseudacorus) since the Middle Ages, is the natural heir of this timeless symbol of true sovereignty: self-mastery. English kings adopted the fleur-de-lys by dint of their medieval claim to the throne of France and the device

Roman goblet (top) and Egyptian water-lily mosaic

can still be seen on our two pence coins (not the deceptively similar ostrich feathers of the Badge of the Prince of Wales, but between the crosses on the coronet from which the plumes sprout).

The blue water-lilies illustrated in the Brislington Villa mosaics are, appropriately, outlined in a stone with a deep blue sheen. And it is notable that they are depicted as opening buds, promising a wondrous revelation in the fullness of time.

Many modern researchers believe that the ancient Egyptians steeped blue water-lily flowers in wine, imparting a euphoric quality to the brew and, no doubt, a certain mystical glow to any festive occasion. Such a popular use could explain the present rarity of the plants in their natural habitat.

The cantharus with its four lilies is on display at Bristol City Museum and Art

---

1. For a remarkable account of early Christianity as a Mystery Religion see Timothy Freke & Peter Gandy, *The Jesus Mysteries*, London, Thorsons, 1999.

Gallery, and portions of the villa's triclinium mosaic (including the lily shown here) can be seen by appointment at the King's Weston Roman Villa museum.

Brislington Villa was destroyed about one hundred years after it was built, probably by Irish raiders, and was rediscovered in 1899 and subsequently excavated.[1] Significantly, among the debris, a variety of Roman household goods and some demolition debris were recovered from its well, which was 11.5 metres deep, along with the skeletal remains of four people.

Prophetic Dreams and the Night Mare

The earliest paranormal event connected with Brislington may be a prophetic dream whose warning was entrusted to Robert Fitzhamon, Lord of the Manor of Brislington.

Robert (c.1064-1107) was a Norman knight who had been given Brislington Manor by his cousin King William II (1057-1100). The king was crowned in September 1087 according to the will of his late father William the Conqueror, and his gift of the Manor to Robert detached Brislington from its earlier position in the extensive manor of Keynsham.

It is not known for certain whether Robert lived in the moated and fortified manor that stood at the bottom of Sturminster Road, or even whether he ever visited this rustic part of his portfolio of assets. Manor Farm, as the house became known, is even of uncertain date, but it surely existed by the early fourteenth century when the rest of the villagers would have dwelt in wattle and daub huts. Its demolition in 1933 made it unlikely that the Saxon features it was thought to incorporate will be verified soon. But Robert's story does at least allow us to glimpse the high regard in which the aristocracy held the paranormal, 900 years ago.

King William's life was a bloody one, and it is debatable whether his byname Rufus 'red' referred to flaming red hair or an incandescent temper. The chronicler Peter of Blois recorded a long series of events that we would term 'acts of God' apparently showing heaven's displeasure with the violence that characterised Rufus's reign. Those celestial signs included lightnings and thunderbolts, and violent winds and whirlwinds that shook and levelled the towers of churches.

The mention of the churches is particularly significant because Rufus was certainly no friend to the Church of Rome and, in some circles at least, he is even regarded as a pagan king, making his untimely death a matter of more than usual controversy. Nevertheless, it was a monk who approached Robert Fitzhamon,

1. W R Barker 1901, *An Account of the Remains of a Roman Villa Discovered at Brislington, Bristol, December 1899*, Bristol, The City Museum.

Lord of Brislington, with concerns over the safety of the king. The monk was deeply troubled by a dream in which he saw the king die whilst out hunting: a prognostication that was soon to come horribly true.[1]

In fact, the king himself may have had a premonition of his doom: on the eve of his death he suffered a dream in which his blood streamed heavenwards and blotted out the sun. We cannot be sure whether Robert had passed on the monk's message, which had triggered the king's own nightmare, but Robert was certainly staying with the king at his court in Winchester at the time. And, following his vision of a day darkened by bloodshed, the king kept vigil through the rest of the night.

On August 2nd, 1100, Rufus went hunting in the New Forest. As he rode, aptly, towards the setting sun, he somehow became separated from his companions, all except for Walter Tirel – the last person to see the king alive.

Rufus was eventually found dead, pierced by an arrow, and Walter – an expert bowman, fled to France. Strangely, perhaps, the affair was officially regarded as merely a tragic accident. Walter was not pursued, and his story – that he had aimed at a stag and the arrow had hit Rufus – was accepted at face value.

That the king's death was a politically motivated assassination is perhaps a reasonable view, but some researches suspect the influence of a more subtle conspiracy. The date of the king's death is regarded as particularly significant: August 2nd is renowned as the Celtic festival of Lammas, the celebration of the cutting of the grain harvest, the date that John Barleycorn dies that we might live.

Some modern authors[2] have hailed Rufus as the last English king to willingly accept sacrifice as part of his belief in dark pagan mysteries.

That the stroke fell so very close to the end of the thirteenth year of his reign is also considered to be highly suggestive: thirteen is a sacred number in witchcraft, especially as a delimiting factor (a traditional coven might not grow beyond thirteen members, for instance, and thirteen lunar months concludes a year).

The stag itself is emblematic of the horned god who is represented by, and whose earthly power is vested in the Lord of the coven. To slay the 'stag' at the end of thirteen cycles, then, would mark an event as inevitable as the transition from one year to the next. Or, to put it another way: 'The King is dead. Long live the King!'

Rufus was not allowed to rest in peace for long in the sanctuary of Winchester Cathedral. In sympathy with the church towers that fell during his reign, Winchester's own tower fell not long after his burial, reputedly in pious disgust at the wickedness of the bones of the king who had no love for the Church.

1. Rev. A Richardson 1898, St Anne's Chapel, Brislington, *Proceedings of the Somersetshire Archaeological & Natural History Society*, XLIV, 188.
2. Notably those inspired by the influential book by Margaret Murray 1931, *The God of the Witches*, Oxford, Oxford University Press.

The sacrificial king theory makes a pleasing story but it produces more questions than answers and has been roundly discredited by modern scholarship. Nevertheless, the memorial at the site of his death at Minstead is still a focus of pilgrimage for many modern pagans.

Another dream to feature a death, or perhaps an actual visit from the deceased, occurred in Brislington much more recently. It is widely attested that the human spirit can project itself at the moment of physical death, and travel any distance to visit loved ones. These visits often occur in dreams that only become significant when news of the death eventually arrives. The following tale however, gives this familiar and comforting circumstance a macabre twist.

Although the facts are reported as true, I have changed the names of the people to protect their privacy.

One night in or around 1991 George woke his wife Sarah when he started tossing and turning and making a great deal of noise in his sleep. He struggled for some time and, with a supreme effort, finally broke free of his ordeal.

As soon as he surfaced he blurted out, 'I had a horrible dream. Mrs Vinnicombe [their neighbour] was holding me down. I couldn't get up. I don't know why.'

As the time was about 4am, despite the disturbing dream, they soon went back to sleep. At around 6.45am the couple were woken again. This time it was by a commotion outside – the sound of upset children next door. They soon learned the cause of the youngsters' distress: their mum, Mrs Vinnicombe, had died that night.

Why the spirit of their next-door neighbour had apparently chosen to visit George, and why she had clung to him so vigorously, is a mystery to Sarah, who told me this story.

Their house can hardly be deemed an ancient epicentre of psychic turbulence: it is part of a brick terrace built on a green-field site around 50 years ago.

It is, however, possible that George was simply the most psychically sensitive person around at the time, and that is why Mrs Vinnicombe found herself drawn to him. Perhaps, as the saying goes, she was literally having difficulty simply 'letting go'. Were it not for the appearance of the recently deceased neighbour, we might suspect his dream was simply a nightmare: it certainly has several of the classic hallmarks. Nightmares are not just scary dreams, they are a distinctive and terrifying class of phenomenon that is investigated by psychologists and parapsychologists alike, under the umbrella term 'sleep paralysis'.

If sleep paralysis was merely a case of waking up and feeling unable to move, it would be bad enough, but it actually comes with a catalogue of other symptoms that are far worse. Most of these unpleasant features are included in an experience that I was lucky – or unlucky – enough to have had while living here in Brislington. The quotations below are from a record I made immediately after the Mare's nocturnal visit in the small hours of May 23rd, 2000.

I was in a deep sleep when I 'awoke sharply with the sensation of being pinned to the bed by ... a sword'. I was lying on my front with a vicious pain in the middle of my back (about level with the bottom of my shoulder blades).

Although not pointed like a rapier, the 'sword' felt about 1.5cm in breadth, and was plenty sharp enough to skewer me. In fact, I felt that 'were I to move, the 'blade' might slip in more easily'; it was, I supposed, momentarily 'blocked by my spine'. Furthermore: 'Had it entered my body it would have plunged straight into my heart.'

The sense of oppression was overwhelming, and the presence of an aggressor was frighteningly real.

'I was frozen, unable yet desperately struggling to raise my right hand in an attempt to do something – anything – to take my attacker off-guard. I could not even cry-out, the only sound I could raise was a quiet, groaning... My attacker was unknown, silent, malevolent, strong, and cruel.'

The whole episode probably lasted less than ten seconds, but was vivid and without any normal dreamlike qualities whatsoever. The pain ceased at the same time I regained the ability to move, and I rolled over straight away. Of course, there was no attacker, no sword, and no wound.

Although slightly unusual in that I was prone rather than supine, this is an almost textbook case of sleep paralysis. The experience of a malevolent presence, the pain, desperation to escape from the clutches of an unseen monster, and the inability to move or even cry out are all classic features of this night-stalking horror. Even the time of the event – between two and three in the morning – is the most common hour for nightmares.

This sort of story is often found in books about hauntings, and many people describe their experiences in terms of being petrified with fear while a ghost sits on their bed. However, the popular fascination for alien abduction has brought a shift in reporting patterns: nowadays it is just as likely that a sufferer will speak about a force-field immobilising their bodies while an alien performs unspeakable experiments on their un-anaesthetised flesh.

In earlier generations the interpretations overlaid on events were different again, but they always reflected the culture of their day: witches, demons or other mythological creatures were believed to be responsible.

Mare comes from an Old English word for an incubus, an evil spirit that squats on the chest of its victims, squeezing the air out of them. The incubus was prominent in medieval demonology in Britain as elsewhere in Europe, and derives its name from a Latin word meaning 'lie on'. Although the incubus accrued a reputation as a male sexual demon preying on women (the succubus being the female equivalent) it is the ability to paralyse and suffocate that are the key identifying features of the true nightmare. Researchers have found parallels from cultures around the globe and throughout history.

The physiological origins of the nightmare are not yet perfectly understood by science, but nocturnal paralysis is a natural state that prevents us from acting-out our dreams. At least one in four of us will suffer an unforgettable visit from the Night Mare; fortunately, the great majority of those who do so will never be troubled again. The website of the University of Waterloo, Canada, offers pages of information and an online questionnaire about sleep paralysis.[1]

Synchronicity

We are all used to surprising coincidences, and sometimes they seem to purposefully cluster around a particular moment in time. The eminent psychiatrist Carl Jung (1875–1961) coined the word synchronicity – 'togetherness in time' – to describe exactly this sort of event.

Whether they happen by chance or destiny, synchronicities often have a profound impact on our lives, as shown by this tale told to me by Denis Plunkett, founder of the British Flying Saucer Bureau.

Denis was visiting Winterbourne Library when the librarian took a telephone call. The caller was phoning on behalf of a society in Brislington hoping to invite Denis to address one of their regular meetings, and had rung the library to enquire whether the librarian could put him in touch with the famous UFO authority.

The librarian promptly handed the phone to Denis, who was indeed not only locally but internationally renowned for his talks on UFOs. Denis started hunting for something to write down the caller's contact details, and the librarian helpfully pointed out a stack of scrap paper.

Later, upon arriving home, he discovered that the slip of scrap paper was a redundant form from the library's records. It referred to a book about the Roswell Autopsy, an incident in the US that is infamous among students of ufology.

1. Dr J A Cheyne, 'Sleep Paralysis and Associated Hypnagogic and Hypnopompic Experiences', http://watarts.uwaterloo.ca/~acheyne/S_P.html [accessed 09.12.02].

This double coincidence struck him deeply, particularly as he had been seriously wondering whether to continue working as the mainstay of the Bureau or to 'pack it up'. With this question nagging in his mind, he returned to the library and started checking through the other slips – and there were more than 500 of them – but not one related to a book about the paranormal in general, let alone UFOs in particular. He felt he had drawn the only winning ticket.

This synchronicity seemed too great for him to ignore and even though the speaking engagement in Brislington failed to materialise, he was moved to persevere in his endeavours to see the UFO phenomenon treated scientifically and openly. He still keeps that slip of paper as a souvenir of a pivotal moment in his life.

Looking back on it, when Dennis told me his story I suppose it must have encouraged me, too. I'd actually spoken to him about UFO activity connected with Brislington, but he didn't know of any. And neither had the half-dozen other experts I'd already contacted. So, hearing a heartening tale must have lifted my spirits and helped me take the next step and – with a little luck and a lot of perseverance – I did eventually find those remarkable stories featured in these pages.

Superstitions and Healers

Many popular superstitions are simply common sense passed on by word of mouth from generation to generation: an obvious example is the prohibition against walking under a ladder. Although some folklorists suggested it might perpetuate an ancient taboo against breaking a holy triangle (made by the ladder, wall and ground), surely the origin of this famous adage lies with the ordinary danger of somebody working overhead dropping something on you.

Another local superstition firmly rooted in nature was recalled by Miss Diddie Williams as being a guiding light to the last squire of Brislington, Alfred Clayfield-Ireland (1851-1923).[1] Miss Williams was brought up at The Chestnuts, Bonville Road, which had a stand of a dozen elm trees in the field in front of the house. These graceful trees were occupied by a large rookery, and she watched in dread each spring as Squire Ireland inspected them. An old superstition held that rooks did not nest in an unsafe elm, so any tree that was shunned by the rooks was doomed to be felled by the squire's men.

How long it took the rooks to learn the tell-tale signs of a dying elm is anybody's guess, but the Squire's actions were a tribute to the keen powers of observation of the people who first recognised and understood the rooks' behaviour.

1. A Small, G Strange & R Davey 1979, *Brislington Not So Long Ago*, 23, Bristol, Brislington School. See also Jonathan Rowe & Diddie Williams 1986, *Bygone Brislington*, 32, Bristol, Brislington Conservation and Amenity Society.

Other signs and omens are less easy to explain by common-or-garden cause and effect. In 1993 Gordon Carey told Jonathan Rowe that his father Harry Carey, a local dairyman who ran Oakenhill Farm, had forecast the outbreak of the Second World War after several white bull calves were born. A supposed link between apparently unconnected events or items is also reported in some healing charms.

Phyllis Dew wrote an article [1] referring to Mr Edgell, a healer living at The Rock, which was once a rather isolated community. He enjoyed a reputation as a wart charmer, and her mother had been to see him. He told her to rub the wart with bacon and secretly bury the meat in her garden. The ritual was duly performed, and the warning against jinxing the treatment (by talking about it to anybody else) was strictly heeded. The charm worked a treat: as the meat rotted away, so too the wart disintegrated and disappeared.

The process of curing warts with raw meat is often described as sympathetic magic, whereby one object has a link of 'sympathy' with another, so that whatever happens to one will affect the other. The Voodoo doll is an extreme example of the destructive power of sympathetic magic, while therapeutic operations such as wart charming demonstrate the benign face of this reputedly impersonal natural force.

The same article mentioned Mrs Mary Ford who also had a cottage in The Rock, with a small walled garden. She was known locally as Granny Ford and although she also employed Mr Edgell's traditional method of curing warts, she was renowned for her herbal remedies.

I asked Jonathan Rowe what he knew about her, and he recalled hearing that her cure for a swollen hand was to 'get a cow pat and bind it up'. He was in no doubt that 'she would have been thought of as a white witch' with a popular reputation for 'positive, spiritual, and medical things'.

Granny Ford died in the early 1930s, and although her cottage was demolished when it became derelict, part of the site is undeveloped and some traces remain. A postcard showing her as an old lady standing at her cottage door, and wearing her customary white apron, was posted in 1916. [2]

Although many traditional herbal remedies have been vindicated by modern medical science, some seem to rely on little more than faith healing. A rational explanation of such apparently miraculous cures has been described as the placebo effect, a well-known medical phenomenon that allows people to be healed even though they are given fake medicine.

How a placebo works remains a mystery but it seems to activate the patient's

1. Phyllis Dew, 1986, 'Memories of The Rock', *The Brislington Bugle*, 4, Autumn 1986, 1.
2. J & D Fisher & M & F Ford 1987, *Bristol in Old Postcards*, Volume Three, 33, Bristol, Reflections of a Bygone Age. See also Judith Chard, Mary Axford Mitchell, & Jonathan Rowe 1995, *Brislington The Archive Photographs Series*, 48, Chalford, Chalford Publishing Company.

own powers of self-healing (perhaps through stimulation of the immune system). Although this sort of process has long been suspected as lying at the heart of hypnosis, recent investigations have found clear physiological changes in the brain during hypnosis. Monitoring during hypnotic trance has revealed unusual patterns of electrical activity that raise intriguing questions about the nature of consciousness and the power and role of the irrational and intuitive aspects of the mind.

Dr Edward Long Fox, who opened the pioneering Brislington House asylum in 1806, was an early investigator of 'animal magnetism', a technique pioneered by Dr Franz Anton Mesmer who is regarded as the father of modern hypnotism. Mesmer had followed Father Maximillian Hell in achieving remarkable effects on patients by manipulating a powerful steel magnet around them. But Mesmer went one step further and discovered that he could apparently reproduce the cures using only the 'magnetism' of his own body, and he developed a procedure that particularly employed hand gestures.

A brief but acrimonious correspondence in the pages of a local newspaper[1] between Dr Fox and Milborne Williams of Brislington indicates that Dr Fox had been one of many British medical professionals inspired in 1788 by Dr Mainauduc, a student of Mesmer.

In 1789 Mr Williams challenged Dr Fox, who was then in his late twenties and practicing at Castle Green, Bristol, to answer a list of seven allegations. He asked Dr Fox to confess whether he had 'endeavour'd to cure Diseases by certain Motions of the Hands and Fingers?' And went on scathingly to enquire 'Have you cur'd ONE Patient by these Operations?'

The physical nature of the cures he had in mind is made clear in the next question. 'Do you think the wonderful Cures said to be perform'd by the Professors of Animal Magnetism, such as dissolving the Stone in the Bladder, removing Obstructions in the Liver, healing Ulcers in the Lungs, Kidneys, etc. etc. etc. are real or imaginary?'

Considering this very public ridicule of his professional conduct and reputation, Dr Fox's reply was remarkably restrained. He said his 'Experimental Enquiry concerning what is called Animal Magnetism, was begun ... with a view to discover the nature of the cause to which its Professors ascribed its effects.' And that 'I ceased from the investigation, having been unable to ascertain that the power alluded to had any existence.'

It is quite likely that Mr Williams' searing criticism early in his career discouraged Dr Fox from pursuing his study of the effects of animal magnetism on the

1. *Sarah Farley's Bristol Journal*, 1789, September 5th, 12th, 19th, and October 10th. See also D P Lindegaard 2000, *Brislington Bulletins* No 5, 1776-1799, 35-36, Bristol, Privately printed.

mind, for which there was striking evidence of a powerful force at work (as opposed to effects on the body, for which evidence was indeed lacking). Had he enjoyed the peace to proceed with this study Dr Fox, who is celebrated for his radically humane treatment of the insane, may well have achieved considerable advances in the fields of holistic and complementary therapies.

In answer to Mr Williams' query whether such cures 'are real or imaginary?' we may note that the benefits of hypnotism such as pain management, appear to be achieved independently of how the hypnotic trance is achieved. Results seem to depend instead on latent powers inherent in the patient's own imagination. A modern practitioner could, therefore, reply with a smile that the cures are simultaneously real and imaginary.

We may note in passing that the church of St Luke has long enjoyed an active healing ministry; indeed, St Luke is patron saint of physicians and surgeons.

The 'lucky' iron horseshoe is another well-known relic of a widespread ancient superstition, and examples can be seen on the doors of several older cottages in Brislington. They are carefully positioned with their tips pointing upwards making a bowl-shaped crescent in which good luck accumulates. While some are located away from public gaze, examples are not too hard to find, and may be seen, for instance, at The Rock and Brookside Road.

Ley Lines

Alfred Watkins coined the term 'ley' believing it to indicate a prehistoric road, and detailed his theory in his highly influential book *The Old Straight Track*, which has been reprinted many times since its first edition in 1925. He conjectured that these characteristically straight tracks would have had markers along their routes: apart from prominent hills and other natural features such as notches in the skyline, these ley markers would have included ritual sites such as stone circles, standing stones, and burial mounds, as well as settlements such as forts.

Moreover, he noted the fact that comparatively modern monuments such as churches were often raised on pagan sacred sites, and included them in his list of possible ley markers. Because many such sites are clearly identified on Ordnance Survey maps, these became the starting point for innumerable amateur investigations into the mysterious ley lines, particularly in the 1960s and 70s.

A glance at a modern OS map shows a great many possible markers around Brislington, but none convincingly seem to produce a straight line with a reasonable number of markers passing through this area. A notable exception is an unusually short line (2.55 kilometres) which connects the church of St Luke, St Anne's Well, and (having crossed the Avon) the chapel at Avonview Cemetery. It is aligned approximately 2.5 degrees to the east of true north.

Although I know of no evidence that St Anne's Well was an object of religious devotion before its medieval heyday, the veneration of the springs at nearby Bath since Celtic times show that such continuity is not out of the question. Likewise, the idea that the medieval church of St Luke was raised upon a pagan foundation is pure speculation but cannot be dismissed out of hand. The Avonview chapel dates only to 1882 but occupies a prominent position on the steep rise above the Avon, with extensive views overlooking the Cotswold Hills to the east, the River Avon to the south, and the Mendips to the west. Such a location may have been the site of an earlier sanctuary or other ley marker.

On the strength of this evidence alone, only the most wildly enthusiastic ley hunter would claim such a line as a good candidate for a ley. However, the line also crosses the medieval packhorse bridge and the adjacent – and possibly earlier – wooden-framed stone-lined ford in the heart of Nightingale Valley: such places are notable markers in Watkins' list. Furthermore, the holy well is situated two-thirds of the way between St Luke's church and Avonview chapel, adding a geometric dimension to the puzzle.

Although many people dismiss Watkins' idea of ancient roads (not least because some seem to ignore steep slopes that even Roman surveyors would have avoided – Avonview is fully 55 metres above the river), ley lines are still attracting attention as lines of natural energy criss-crossing the Earth's surface. With this in mind it could also be seen as significant that St Luke's, the holy well, and the bridge are reputedly haunted – perhaps the increased energy from the ley has helped to activate or maintain them.

A further, final tease is provided by one of the memorials clustering around Avonview chapel – the tombstone of Henry Hodge who died in 1912. The beautifully sculpted stone depicts a wreathed druid with a flowing beard standing beneath an oak tree, and carrying a ceremonial sickle. The stone was erected by the United Ancient Order of Druids, and bears the motto UNITAS PAX CONCORDIA, translated as Unity, Peace, Harmony.

An ancient trackway involving an alignment of local ancient monuments has been proposed by Mike Hansford[1] who suggests a route from the high earthwork at Maes Knoll (commonly known as The Tump, at the eastern arm of Dundry Hill), along Fortfield Road (Whitchurch), through Brislington Villa, to St Anne's Well. Although he does not call this a ley line, confining his discussion to

---

1. Mike Hansford 1996 and 2003, www.wansdyke21.org.uk/wansdyke/visitmike.htm [accessed 17.05.05].

the former existence of a Celtic and/or Roman trackway, in every significant way it does fit with the traditional notion of a ley – except that it does not conform to a precisely straight route. But then, many modern dowsers claim the straight lines drawn on maps are actually illusions, and that the true energy lines meander around as they connect the sites – rather like the serpents coiling around the staff on the Caduceus of Hermes.

The possible old straight track linking Keynsham Abbey with St Anne's has been explored in our consideration of The Elms.

UFO Sightings
Arnos Court Park

People are still speculating about a natural explanation for Brislington's most sensationalised UFO sighting. The event was undoubtedly mysterious enough to warrant its inclusion in the local newspaper, but the identity of the witness reporting the incident made it front page news[1] and even gave it national coverage[2] – he was a vicar.

At 9.20 on the evening of April 27th, 1968 the incumbent of St Christopher's Church, Hampstead Road, was strolling with his wife through nearby Arnos Court Park when they saw something that would temporarily shatter the tranquillity of their ministry in the parish.

They were standing near the tree-lined wall alongside Kings Road when, in the deepening twilight, they saw a dome shaped light some 75 metres away toward Holy Souls cemetery, on the far side of a pond.[3] The reverend described the object as floating about two metres above the ground, and being approximately four metres in height and three metres in diameter. The dome was symmetrical, remained in one position, seemed to revolve slowly, and was translucent – the skyline was visible through it. The outer rim or shell was a brownish yellow and was described as being like a very fine framework that seemed somehow volatile. The bright interior was off-white in colour and its light pulsed irregularly.

He also mentioned that the dome contained a central, dark pillar some 1.3 metres high, and this feature led to some very sensational conjecture. Arthur Shuttlewood, a well-known authority on UFOs, not only commented that there were UFO sightings at his home town of Warminster that same night, but suggested that the dark shape in the middle of the glowing craft could have been the figure of a living being – a ufonaut.

The couple had been watching it for around twenty seconds when it simply

1. *The New Observer* (Keynsham edition), May 2nd 1968.
2. Sqdn.Ldr Alastair Prevost 1968, 'Sighting in a Bristol Park', *Flying Saucer Review*, 14, 4, 3. The sighting also received coverage in the *Daily Mirror*.
3. This is now a leaky concrete depression, frequented by skateboarders and young cyclists.

faded completely away. No marks were found on the grass, and there had been no noise throughout. It was the day of the New Moon, so there was no possibility of any hazy moon on the horizon to account for the luminous dome.

The dome-shaped Arnos Court Park UFO

The vicar reported the sighting to the police, his bishop, and the local press; which started something of a media circus that blighted the family and upset the congregation for some considerable time.

Some people still believe the light was merely a cloud of luminous gas exhaled from the adjoining cemeteries of Arnos Vale and Holy Souls – it was a warm and humid spring evening after a day of steady rain (the sky was mostly clear at the time of the sighting), and there was negligible wind. So, was this a Will o' the Wisp or an alien making contact?

It is perfectly understandable that the principle witness offered another interpretation, one consistent with his own beliefs, and he quoted Ephesians 6:12 as a possible explanation – the verse refers to the Christians' spiritual struggle against an evil multitude from the heavens.

Oddly, there was also a report[1] that some teenagers had seen a similar object about five years previously; it was in the same place, and also around 9pm on a Saturday night. Plucking up courage, they approached it but the light intensified scaring them so much that one ran home in tears.

Trelawney Park

On the Sunday following the Arnos Court Park sighting, Mrs Anderson saw a UFO from the window of her bedroom in Trelawney Park. It was about 4.10am on May 5th, 1968, and she was sitting up in bed wide awake when she saw a bright yellow spherical object that had a tail trailing behind it. It flew slowly, just above the rooftops, and seemed to be heading in the direction of Arnos Court Park. It disappeared from her view after five to ten seconds, and was completely silent. She described it as about the size of a football held at arm's length.[2]

Kensington Park

A lifelong fascination with astronomy has given Joules Taylor a good familiarity with the night sky but in all her years of observing the heavens, she has never seen anything like the object she saw from the rear garden of her home in the Kensington Park area of Brislington.

1. *Flying Saucer Review*, 14, 4, 4.
2. *Ibid*. This was also reported on the front page of *The New Observer* (Keynsham edition), May 9th 1968.

It was midnight in mid-October 1993 (or, possibly, 1992) and the Milky Way was clearly visible. She was enjoying the spectacle when her attention was caught by a dark shape steadily crossing the bright band of stars in or near the constellation of Cepheus.

The shape was 'hard edged' and black, 'darker than the sky', and had no distinguishing features or lights of any kind. She is positive about the shape of craft's leading edge: the illustration (based on her own drawing) shows that it was not dissimilar to the silhouette of the pointed end of half a lemon, the point being the craft's nose cone. But she is uncertain about the shape of the trailing edge.

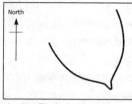

Joules Taylor's Kensington Park UFO

The distance between its wingtips has been calculated to be at least three degrees of arc, which means that if it had the wingspan of an Airbus jetliner, its height would have been just 600 metres, but there was no sound of aircraft noise (the neighbourhood is under the flight path of many planes using local airport, so such sounds are all too easily recognised). If the craft was higher it must have been correspondingly larger: potentially even a mothership of enormous size.

She said: 'Once it moved away from the Milky Way it was difficult to see.' Indeed, after five or six seconds she lost track of it, but for the time it was under observation it maintained a straight path heading towards the south-southwest.

Triangular craft with 'impossible' characteristics have been seen innumerable times, particularly in the late 1980s and 1990s. Some have been debunked as hi-tech military stealth planes from the United States (many ufologists cite the Aurora project as the tip of a covert iceberg), but a core of sightings such as this one describe aspects of the craft that remain the stuff of science fiction.

Bath Road

Opposite the independent television studios is a fast-food restaurant outside of which local resident Mark Thompson witnessed an unidentified flying object in 2001.[1] It was early evening, perhaps about 7pm, around the middle of September when the resplendent red western clouds of sunset attracted his attention. But Mark saw more than he expected, something beyond the scope of normal experience.

His first thought was that he was seeing a helium-filled party balloon, but he soon realised that it wasn't simply floating in the air: it moved as if it were a

 1. Mark Thompson c.2002, www.ufosightingsuk.co.uk/display_sightings.asp?searchcounty=3 [accessed 23.01.04].

pendulum bob swinging gracefully in a circle.

The object was a dull metallic orb, smooth, and slightly flattened, and it reflected the light from the setting sun. Its motion took it periodically behind a big cumulus cloud for several seconds. Mark was able to estimate the height of the cloud to be about three kilometres, which would, he figured, make the object comparable in size to a large jet airliner.

The sighting lasted for maybe five minutes or so; long enough for him to think of dashing home and bringing his wife out to see it. Unfortunately the object had disappeared by the time he returned to look for it. But there were certainly other people around at the time who may also have seen it.

Mark reckoned the incident to have been so strange that he was wrote a thorough account of it, and he submitted it to public scrutiny in the website archives of UFO Sightings in the UK, one of Britain's more reputable internet resources devoted to the study of ufology.

The precise direction in which the object was seen is unknown, although it may well have been over Arnos Vale Cemetery. An ancient theory proposes that certain psychic hot-spots (and some people may consider Arnos Vale Cemetery to be one) can cause a sort of etheric-lensing that brings the otherwise invisible and intangible into view. Ley lines and the phenomenon of the genius loci are associated aspects of this idea, as indeed are the appearances of fabulous beasts ...

A Fantasy of Unicorns

There is something romantic about unicorns, and when they come to visit you it would be the very height of bad manners to ignore them. For several years in the mid-1990s, I found myself almost tripping over them and I took the opportunity to photograph the less fleeting ones.

These unicorn photographs are, of course, the sheerest nonsense (since when were magical beings obliged to make sense?) but one is included here to illustrate a rather important point. It is common knowledge that we all tend to see what we want to see, and literally overlook the rest, but many people are keen to un-blinker themselves and see things for what they really are. There are many techniques for developing this clearer sight – clairvoyance – and one of the best is simply to pay attention to the way things make you feel.

The connection between the objects around us and the emotions they inspire within us is powerful and all pervasive, and it can be very enlightening to observe it in action. Advertisements and public relations campaigns wouldn't

A heavenly cherub?

be funded if they didn't produce a substantial return on investment; and many work by manipulating our reactions to carefully selected stimuli. Freeing ourselves from such commercial exploitation may be one goal of becoming more sensitive to our environment, but it is really a milestone on the road to self-discovery and empowerment.

We all know how easy it is to fall prey to bad dreams when we are stressed and acting against our nature, but the opposite is also true: we can all change our dreams and our lives for the better. Just as our dreams can reflect and reveal our inner state, we can learn to recognise signs in everyday life that can help us steer towards our heart's desire. Imagine life is like a Rorschach inkblot test, where we all see wonderful or hideous things emerging from a perfectly innocent pattern on a blank canvas. Learning to see our own hopes and fears for what they are is a hallmark of true clairvoyance.

The children's game of seeing mountains, castles, dragons and faces in clouds is another technique for exploring our own subconscious mind. Simply taking the time to enjoy this sort of daydreaming, relaxing on a summer's afternoon, can both combat stress and even allow deeply buried memories and insights to well up into consciousness. This sort of process, incidentally, lies at the heart of many ancient forms of divination, and is akin to the best dream interpretations. The object of any true oracle is to help make us aware of something valuable or important, allowing us to make an informed decision.

Opening up better communication with the deeper levels of our mind can bring us a profoundly increased sense of personal well-being and inner strength. Many researchers into the paranormal believe that it also offers the best way to nurture innate psychic abilities.

So the next time you see the face of Jesus in a stain under a flowerpot, or see the yin/yang symbol in the moon, or hear an old flame's name whispered on the wind; don't just shrug it off. Give yourself time to consider your feelings – let them rise and reveal themselves. Perhaps you won't have a blinding flash of inspiration, but you might just find yourself adding a vital piece to a larger jigsaw, so savour the moment.

A unicorn?

It is vital, of course, to remember that it is perfectly natural for people to find signs and see visions that use the symbolism of their own particular faith. In a multicultural society we are well-placed to search for the underlying essence and not to be distracted by their surface appearance.

Both this unicorn (actually a wad of hair) and the Heavenly Cherub cumulus cloud were photographed in Brislington, along with a good many others.

Index   Figures in **bold** indicate illustrations